WINTERS HIGH SCHOOL LIBRARY

D0531848

DISCARDED

African-Americans &
THE PRESIDENCY
A HISTORY OF BROKEN PROMISES

African-Americans & THE PRESIDENCY

A HISTORY OF BROKEN PROMISES

Christopher B. Booker

Franklin Watts
A Division of Grolier Publishing
New York · London · Hong Kong · Sydney
Danbury, Connecticut

TO MY MOTHER, RENA A. BOOKER

Frontispiece: President Abraham Lincoln entering Richmond, Virginia, in April 1865

Photographs ©: Archive Photos: 77 (Matthew Brady), 38, 50, 83 (Kean), 10, 59, 84, 86, 102, 129, 133; Corbis-Bettmann: 31 (Leonard de Selva), 159 (Martin Jeong/UPI), 152 (L. Mark/UPI), 116 (Jack Moebes), 161 (Cliff Owen/UPI), 162 (Reuters Newmedia, Inc.), 108 (Grant Smith), 94, 110 (UPI), 13, 19, 40, 45, 55, 65, 68, 70, 90, 92, 101, 103, 118, 121, 128, 135, 137, 142, 147, 154; Courtesy of Photodisc, Inc.: cover; Jimmy Carter Library: 145; John F. Kennedy Library: 126; Library of Congress: 2.

Book design by Vicki Fischman

Visit Franklin Watts on the Internet at:
http://www.publishing.grolier.com

Library of Congress Cataloging-in-Publication Data

Booker, Christopher B., 1949–
    African-Americans and the presidency : a history of broken promises / Christopher B. Booker.
      p. cm.
    Includes biographical references and index.
    ISBN 0-531-11882-7
    1. Presidents—United States—Racial attitudes—Juvenile literature.
    2. Afro-Americans—Politics and government—Juvenile literature.
    3. Afro-Americans—Civil rights—History—Juvenile literature.
    4. United States—Race relations—Juvenile literature. 5. United States—Politics and government—Juvenile literature. [1. Presidents—Racial attitudes.
    2. Afro-Americans—Politics and government. 3. Afro-Americans—Civil rights—History. 4. United States—Race relations—Juvenile literature. 5. United States—Politics and government.] I. Title.

E176.1.B73 2000
973'.09'9—dc21   00-035204

© 2000 by Christopher B. Booker
All rights reserved. Published simultaneously in Canada
Printed in the United States of America
1 2 3 4 5 6 7 8 9 10 R 09 08 07 06 05 04 03 02 01 00

CONTENTS

African-Americans &
THE PRESIDENCY
A HISTORY OF BROKEN PROMISES

THE FOUNDING FATHERS AND AFRICANS IN AMERICA

Indeed I tremble for my country when I reflect that God is just: that his justice cannot sleep forever: that considering numbers, nature and natural means only, a revolution of the wheel of fortune, an exchange of situation, is among possible events: that it may become probable by supernatural interference! The Almighty has no attribute which can take side with us in such a contest.

—Thomas Jefferson[1]

AFRICAN ENSLAVEMENT IN COLONIAL AMERICA

By 1619 when the first captives from Africa landed in Jamestown, Virginia, the modern slave trade had been in existence for more than a century and a half.[2] The fabulous wealth gained from the land and indigenous people of the Americas and Africa, as well as the outright plunder of nonhuman resources, fueled the economic development of both North

Slavery was a brutal reality during the Colonial period and for years to come.

America and Europe.[3] Profits from the slave trade alone helped finance the British Industrial Revolution. One resident of Bristol, a port developed by virtue of the trade in Africans, said, "There was not a brick in the city but was cemented with the blood of a slave."[4] There was "blood" aplenty in the trade— often on both sides—and at least one European power halted the slave trade temporarily due to the bloody slave revolts that took quite a toll on the slavers. It is estimated that there were 150 recorded rebellions by the captured Africans on the high seas. The toll of African death and misery during the passage across the Atlantic was incredibly high: an estimated one-third of the millions of captives died while at sea. Another one-third died during the seasoning process in the Caribbean or on the North American mainland.[5]

Slave insurrection—a great fear shared by slave owners in early American history—was particularly evident during the Colonial period. The black struggle for freedom quickened its pace as the new ideology of liberty, spawned by the white American fight against their British Colonial rulers, permeated the thirteen colonies of North America. On January 6, 1773, Africans petitioned Governor Hutchinson of Massachusetts, plainly protesting the fact that "every Day of their Lives [are] imbittered (*sic*) with this most intollerable (*sic*) Reflection, That, let their Behavior be what it will, nor their Children to all Generations, shall ever be able to do, or to possess and enjoy any Thing, no not even Life itself. . . ." The enslaved blacks decried this legal and official social status that attempted to reduce them to the level of beasts. "We have no Property! We have no Wives! No Children! We have no City! No Country! . . ."[6] In 1774, Abigail Adams, wife of John Adams, the second president of the United States, wrote her husband expressing fears about "a conspiracy of the negroes" in town. This "conspiracy" involved petitioning the governor for freedom. More antislavery than her husband, she expressed her heartfelt desire that "there was not a slave in the province; it always appeared a most iniquitous scheme to me to fight ourselves for what we are daily robbing and plundering from those who have as good a right to freedom as we have."[7] Patrick Henry, whose slogan, "Give me Liberty or give me Death!" energized the American independence movement, said, "Every thinking honest man rejects slavery in Speculation, how few in practice? Would anyone believe that I am Master of slaves of my own purchase? I am drawn along by the general inconvenience of living without them; I will not, I cannot justify it."[8] Others thought it strange too. During the 1770s, Samuel Johnson wondered aloud, "How is it that we hear the loudest yelps for liberty from the drivers of Negroes?"[9] The American colonists ironically spoke of the horror of being reduced to slavery by the British.

The reaction of Patrick Henry to Lord Dunmore's offer of emancipation to Africans willing to fight in the British Army was typical. Henry termed the proclamation "fatal to the publick (*sic*) Safety," and called for stricter steps to keep blacks from fleeing or rising.[10] During one incident, "Jerry," a harbor pilot, was hanged and burned in South Carolina for the crime of helping fellow Africans obtain arms in order to flee slavery.[11]

GEORGE WASHINGTON AND AFRICAN SLAVERY

George Washington was born in February 1732 in Westmoreland County, Virginia. During his childhood, George often played with enslaved African children on his father's plantation. Later, as custom dictated, the playmates were separated in order that George could be reared as a master and they as slaves.[12] George Washington's father, Augustine Washington, received 11,000 acres (4,451 hectares) of land from the colonial administration. Marrying Jane Butler, the sixteen-year-old daughter of another wealthy settler, he was well prepared to enhance his wealth from an early age. By speculating in land, acquiring sinecures, raising tobacco, and working slaves, he prospered.[13] After his first wife died, Augustine remarried. It was his second wife, Mary, with whom he had his son George.

At the time of the future president's birth, his family owned approximately twenty slaves and several thousand acres. However, George's father, Augustine, died when he was only 49 and George was 11. Young George then fell under the influence of his powerful neighbors, the Fairfaxes. Following a brief stint in

As a plantation owner, George Washington was master to many slaves.

the colony's military force, he returned to civilian status. At that time, Washington owned 49 Africans as slaves.[14] His holdings of slaves and land dramatically increased following his marriage to Virginia's richest widow, Martha Custis, who had inherited 100 slaves and 6,000 acres (2,400 ha) from her planter husband.[15] Thereafter Washington constantly sought to augment his force of enslaved blacks, often shopping for bargain slaves on the Maryland side of the Potomac. Washington paid taxes on 49 slaves in 1760, 78 in 1765, 87 in 1770, 135 in 1775, 216 in 1786, and by 1799, he had 317 slaves spread over five plantations.[16]

There is scant evidence that Washington was an exceptionally kind slave master. For example, he responded harshly to the desire for liberty among the Africans he claimed to own. Washington's letter to Captain Josiah Thompson read: "Sir, with this letter comes a Negro (Tom) which I beg the favor of you to sell, in any of the Islands you may go to, for whatever he will fetch. . . ." asking in return several commodities including rum, limes, and molasses.[17] Washington said the African was "both a rogue and a runaway," commenting that he was "by no means" unique in this respect. Washington, focusing upon the price his captive would command on the market, stressed that "Tom" was "exceedingly strong and healthy, and good at the hoe," and possessed management skills as a foreman. He warned Captain Thompson, however, that he should be sure to keep him handcuffed until he reached the sea.[18]

Washington's strategy to administer his plantations relied on the routine intimidation and degrees of terror common to the institution of slavery. While he did not want his overseers to be completely without mercy, he did desire that they provide sufficient incentive for blacks to work as hard as their physical condition would allow. If an African had less arduous work duties and was thought to be malingering, he or she was to be threatened with being made into a "common hoe negro," a field slave. If he thought it necessary, Washington had his slaves whipped. Runaway slaves were hunted down with dogs and severely flogged when captured.[19]

In 1792, Washington ordered his subordinates not to waste money on sick slaves considered too unproductive to be useful to him. He was inclined to believe that they were feigning illness, contending that their ailments came from their propensity to "night walk" rendering them "unfit for the duties of the day."[20] Washington ordered his slaves to "work from daybreaking (*sic*) until it is dusk.." Fearing that they would be "ruined by idleness," he ordered his managers to "let them be employed in any manner . . . that will keep them out of idleness and mischief. . . ."

Of his house slaves, Washington wrote that he knew "of no black person about the house that is to be trusted." His wife, Martha, not surprisingly, shared a similar outlook. After loaning a slave to a niece, she wrote that she hoped "you will not find in him much sass. [T]he Blacks are so bad in their nature that they have not the least gratitude for the kindness that may be showed to them."[21]

One domestic slave, Oney Judge, was considered to be pampered by the Washingtons, but she fled, seeking her freedom. Washington's response in his attempts to reclaim his "property" suggests that he failed to comprehend the basic human impulse toward liberty. As a result of the power of the northern anti-slavery movement and the African urban community, Washington's slave catcher could not seize Judge without setting off a riot. Oney Judge thus won her emancipation from the Father of the Country. The escape to freedom from Washington's slavery was not unique to Oney Judge, however, as several other Washington-owned Africans did likewise.[22]

Washington was once visited by an English traveler who concluded that the former president was not "of a humane disposition."[23] When Polish revolutionary Julian Ursyn Niemcewicz toured Washington's Mount Vernon plantation, he was appalled at the misery of the conditions for black slaves.[24] Yet he concluded that Washington treated blacks better than other slaveholders in the area.

The evidence suggests that Washington's treatment of his slaves was well within the normal range of contemporary slave owners. One winter, Africans on one of Washington's plantations felt compelled to plead for more food. In another instance, one October he grew irritated at their requests for blankets. The validity of their complaints is buttressed by the fact that during the following spring Washington admitted that he had "lost more Negroes last winter" than he had in years.[25]

In 1791, Washington began to fear that his ownership of the slaves who lived with him in Philadelphia was in jeopardy since he had lived in the city for so many years. Besides the question of his legal right to ownership, he was preoccupied by the worry that his slaves would be "enticed" away to their misfortune. Even without their escape, Washington feared that any chance of freedom might "ruin" them, making them "insolent in a state of slavery."[26] Hence, Washington ordered that his domestic slaves be spirited back to his Mount Vernon, Virginia plantation where they would be secure in slavery. Washington's action came too late; Hercules, a cook, fled while in Philadelphia. Washington suffered in the cook's absence, for he had become completely dependent on his slave for cooking. After experiencing difficulty in replacing him, Washington was tempted to risk his reputation and attempt to recapture the cook. Finally, he resolved the problem by hiring a white person to cook for him.[27]

Washington had several opportunities to demonstrate the sincerity of his oft-noted antislavery remarks. Irritated in 1786 by abolitionist efforts to free an African held by one of his Alexandria neighbors on a trip to Pennsylvania, Washington said that his opposition to this Quaker action didn't mean "that I wish to hold these unhappy people . . . in slavery." Washington went on, ". . . no man living wishes more sincerely than I do to see the abolition of it."[28] Earlier, after Washington expressed enthusiasm for Lafayette's plan to buy an estate to experiment with free African labor, he postponed the plan and nothing came of it.[29] Emancipation for Washington's African slaves was to come with his wife's death. Washington's will immediately emancipated the "Mulatto man," William Lee, specifying that Lee could remain if he desired and that he be given a $30 annuity for his retirement.[30] For those too old to work, the former president provided that they "shall be comfortably clothed and fed by my heirs while they live. . . ." The younger slaves would remain in bondage until the age of 25, being taught to both read and write and a trade.[31]

JOHN ADAMS: NON-SLAVE-OWNING PRESIDENT

The Federalist Party's John Adams, the second president and the only non-slave-owner among the early American presidents, was born in Braintree, now Quincy, Massachusetts. Massachusetts had approximately 5,000 African slaves during the late Colonial era.[32] Sam Adams, the future president's cousin, had at least one domestic slave and it is likely that John Adams was personally connected to slavery in other ways. Beginning at Harvard in 1751, Adams embarked upon a career that saw him rise to become one of the most prominent Founding Fathers of the new nation of the United States. Prior to the Revolution— after Crispus Attucks, an enslaved African "fugitive," fell as the first person slain by the British in the American Revolution— John Adams was charged with the task of prosecuting the case for the British crown. He accused Attucks of being in a "mob," "a motley rabble of saucy boys, negroes and molattoes (sic), Irish teagues and outlandish jack-tarrs. . . ."[33] After the movement for independence gained momentum, however, Adams, who had switched sides and now opposed the British, wrote a protest note to Governor Thomas Hutchinson in 1773 and did not hestitate to sign it with the name of the martyr "Crispus Attucks"—which by then held powerful symbolic significance for the independence movement.[34]

In his 1800 presidential campaign against Thomas Jefferson, Adams's Federalist supporters charged not only that Jefferson was a thief, a coward, and a cheat, but "a mean-spirited, low-lived fellow, the son of a half-breed Indian squaw, sired by a Virginia mulatto father . . ."[35] Jefferson's defeat of Adams, 73 electoral votes to 65, was in all probability due to the constitutional feature granting the South a three-fifths vote for each enslaved African. Without this bolstered southern political strength, Adams would in all likelihood have won.[36]

THOMAS JEFFERSON: SLAVEHOLDER REVOLUTIONARY

The earliest memory held by Thomas Jefferson was of being handed to and carried by an African slave in Virginia.[37] Until he was nine years old, Jefferson was immersed in a world that included dozens of African children; more than 100 slaves were kept on his Tuckahoe plantation. The children played on the margins of a cruel world characterized by the routine terror of slavery.

Thomas Jefferson inherited a long family history of involvement with slavery. His grandfather, Isham Randolph, for example, was a slave trader. By age 14, Thomas Jefferson was given a slave as a body servant and valet, and he continued to rely upon one for the rest of his life. When Jefferson reached the age of 21, he inherited 2,500 acres (1,010 ha) and 30 African slaves and stood to gain 2,500 additional acres (1,010 ha) upon his mother's death. Shortly after his marriage to Martha Skelton, she inherited 135 slaves.[38]

Jefferson professed to abhor slavery more than anyone, but he maintained that he could not afford to free his slaves until he "cleared off" some of his debts. Following this, Jefferson promised to do something to make "their situation happier"—short of emancipating them. Emancipation was out of the question because he truly believed that the "Negro race [was] . . . made to carry burthens (sic)."[39] In addition, during the years after 1773, Jefferson increasingly voiced his fears of "racial mixture" as a cause for the degradation of the white race.[40]

In his practical actions, Jefferson was consistent in his defense of slave owners. For example, Washington's attitude

Thomas Jefferson overseeing one of the dozens of slaves he owned throughout his lifetime

toward the use of black troops in the American Revolutionary War was clear: He banned them from the army initially. In contrast, Jefferson's views were less clear; he feared arming Africans, who he knew desperately wanted freedom from enslavement. While Jefferson supported the recruitment of Africans in Virginia, he refused to offer them freedom in return for their sacrifices. Hence, many were attracted by Lord Dunmore's offer of emancipation in return for enlistment in the British Army. This offer earned Dunmore the burning hatred of American revolutionaries such as Jefferson. Undermining a slave owner's authority over slaves was regarded as perhaps the lowest, most morally reprehensible act possible, since it betrayed the bonds of racial loyalty existing between the Americans and the English.[41] Thirty of Jefferson's slaves escaped to the British, while thousands of others in Virginia took advantage of the disunity among whites to free themselves. Jefferson himself estimated that approximately 30,000 Africans escaped slavery and joined the British during the war.[42]

During the 1783–1794 period, Jefferson sold approximately 50 Africans as slaves in order to maintain his lavish lifestyle and to repay a debt.[43] More recent writers have estimated that during the 10-year span from 1784 to 1794, Jefferson sold 161 Africans.[44] The idea of breeding humans for profit did not repulse Jefferson, who once said while giving his overseer orders, "I consider the labor of a breeding woman as no object, and that a child raised every two years is of more profit than the crop of the best laboring man. In this, as in all other cases, Providence has made our interests and our duties coincide perfectly. . . ."[45]

It is difficult to gain an accurate glimpse behind the curtain of secrecy the slave owners drew around the micro-societies on their plantations. However, there is evidence that Jefferson, like almost all his fellow slaveholders, could rise to great heights of cruelty and sink to the depths of callous greed. In one instance, James Hubbard, an African slave, ran away and upon his capture was whipped. Jefferson commented that he "had him severely flogged in the presence of his old companions," illustrating the routine cruelty on the Jefferson plantation.[46]

Like other slaveholders, Jefferson could not bear the thought of a free black community existing side-by-side with a free white community. Hence, the emancipation of blacks was inconceivable unless it was accompanied by emigration. Jefferson feared that black memories of the horrors of slavery, white prejudice, and innate racial distinctions would combine to produce social convulsions that would eventually lead to white or black "extermination."[47]

In Jefferson's perception, the "real distinction" made by nature resulted in blacks being distinctly inferior. Black emigration was necessary, in part, to avoid a mixture of races that would pollute the white race, fouling its beauty and intellect. He thought the "fine mixtures of red and white" more attractive than "that immoveable (*sic*) veil of black," citing the whites' "flowing hair" and "more elegant symmetry of form." Jefferson felt proof of this could be found in the blacks' own perception of whites as more physically attractive.[48]

Jefferson enjoyed many friends and acquaintances among the circles of European revolutionary republicans. In 1796, one of Jefferson's French republican friends visited him at his plantation, Monticello. The famous Comte de Volney was astonished to see slaves, particularly some white-appearing slave children, living in horrible conditions.[49] Jefferson was sensitive and embarrassed about his slaveholding status and allowed outsiders only a glimpse into the conditions that existed on his Monticello plantation.

Jefferson's scandal involving Sally Hemings blossomed from a story written by the well-known journalist James Thomson Callender, who felt that Jefferson had been ungrateful to him for past deeds of service. Passed over for the position of postmaster, Callender first wrote of President Jefferson's relationship with Sally Hemings in 1802. Callender's stories revealed that the president kept a black "concubine," who had given birth to a son strongly resembling him. The journalist wrote that if the president's example were emulated among the lesser white men of Virginia the state would be completely overrun by "mulattoes," leading to a civil war, massacres, and the eventual extermination of blacks and mulattoes.[50] Callender boldly accused Jefferson of flouting a norm that was formerly one of the most sacred among slaveholders. For a man of Jefferson's prominence, the accusation was especially serious since he was charged not only with having sex with his slave but of maintaining a form of marital relationship, thereby threatening the whole structure of race relations connected to American slavery. Jefferson's response was largely to remain silent and allow the controversy to eventually fade.

Jefferson's views on racial equality were multidimensional and complex. In his *Notes on Virginia*, Jefferson wrote unfavorably of black intellect, asserting that in memory "they are equal to the white," in "reason much inferior," and "in imagination they are dull, tasteless, and anomalous."[51]

Maryland's Benjamin Bannecker was an American-born African mathematician, surveyor, and astronomer. He had for years sought to use the reality of his personal achievements to advance the cause of black freedom. His goal was to demonstrate the heights that Africans could attain intellectually, even while hampered by a pervasive racism that hemmed in every aspect of their lives. Between 1792 and 1797, Bannecker published six almanacs in 28 editions that were widely distributed in the major cities along the eastern seaboard.

In 1791, Jefferson approved Bannecker's appointment as an assistant to Andrew Ellicott, who was to survey the newly planned American capital. Later that year, Bannecker wrote a letter to Jefferson, who was then U.S. secretary of state. In a bold and courageous challenge to perhaps the most prominent living American, Bannecker expressed the hope that Jefferson would "readily embrace every opportunity" to destroy the "absurd and false ideas" contending that Africans were intellectually inferior. Bannecker told the future president that he was proud of his African heritage and realized his good fortune at not being yoked in the chains of slavery. In the letter, he frankly stated "how pitiable" it is that a man "so fully convinced of the benevolence" of God should "counteract his mercies, in detaining by fraud and violence so numerous a part of my brethren under groaning captivity and cruel oppression. . . ."[52]

Bannecker continued to advise Jefferson to "wean" himself from "narrow prejudices" and to abide by a moral stricture akin to the Golden Rule. Bannecker finally presented Jefferson with the gift of his almanac, recounting that it was produced under many "difficulties and disadvantages." Jefferson thanked Bannecker for the almanac and promised to examine it as he desired but repeatedly stated his doubts that blacks were equal despite his most fervent desire that they be so. He wrote about Bannecker to Joel Barlow three years after Bannecker's death:

We know he had spherical trigonometry enough to make almanacs, but not without the suspicion of aid from Ellicott, who was his neighbor and friend, and never missed an opportunity of puffing him. I have a long letter from Banneker, which shows him to have had a mind of very common stature indeed. . . .[53]

Jefferson also dismissed the talents of black poet Phillis Wheatley. Although he had earlier confessed an inability to critically judge poetry, he confidently pronounced the "compositions published under her name" as "beneath the dignity" of his consideration.[54] Wheatley's work was defended, in contrast, by such prominent European critics as Voltaire.[55]

Jefferson's views on slavery were shaped in part by his financial dependence on the institution. His position against black emancipation hardened as time went on, and he opposed even the most timid efforts to launch a gradual abolition, to foster improvements in the African condition within slavery, or to allow the federal government minimal power to regulate slavery as an institution.

Late in life, Jefferson embraced the "states' rights" position used by defenders of slavery—and, later, of Jim Crow laws that promoted discrimination—to argue against federal intervention. Jefferson's fear of any possible federal plan to emancipate African slaves is indicative of the real strength of his stated desire for black emancipation. Any such scenario, he warned, would be catastrophic. He foresaw the wholesale evacuation of "all the whites south of the Potomac and Ohio" and "most fortunate those who can do it first." With their freedom, he maintained, the blacks would be given a dagger that they would not hesitate to use on whites.[56] Jefferson's prophetic writing concerning the coming of the Civil War suggests that he would have sided with Jefferson Davis and the Confederacy.[57]

As an elder statesman in the twilight of his years, Jefferson joined with his Virginia neighbors Madison and Monroe to advocate the colonization of blacks. In his final words on the subject, Jefferson wrote in favor of an improbable strategy: a federally funded gradual program of black removal to a nearby foreign land. Africans born after a certain date would be deported when they reached a predetermined age. Those born before that date would be allowed to stay. He admitted that this would be a very slow process, but he believed that this was the beauty of the plan.[58] At the age of 82, Marquis de Lafayette visited Jefferson at Monticello one last time. He urged the former president to participate in a modest plan to educate African slaves as a step toward their emancipation. Jefferson insisted that the time for black liberty was not yet ripe, recalling his lifelong fear that any mention of possible black emancipation might tighten the chains of slavery even more. Jefferson did, however, endorse the call to educate blacks, with one exception. He felt it was acceptable for black slaves to learn to read, but not to write. Jefferson's logic was that with writing they would be able to forge papers and could possibly escape to freedom.[59] In this manner, Jefferson, to the end, supported the actual enslavement of his fellow humans and actively engaged his powerful intelligence in securing the chains of their oppression.

JAMES MADISON: EMBARRASSED SLAVEHOLDER

The fourth president of the United States, James Madison, was also raised on a Virginia slave plantation. As the male offspring of an upwardly mobile slave-owning family, the sickly Madison attended Princeton in the 1770s. Following his graduation, he returned home to Orange County, Virginia, and became involved in the political scene during a period of rapidly increasing anti-Colonial agitation. Madison's key role in the American Revolution, his *Federalist Papers*, and his role at the Constitutional Convention have made him one of the most venerated Founding Fathers. Like Jefferson, he was embarrassed by his ownership of African slaves since it appeared to be an obvious contradiction of his revolutionary humanist convictions.[60]

By the early 1780s, the Madison family possessed more than 100 slaves, and its Montpelier plantation had more slaves than any other in the county. Madison depended on slave labor for his income and admittedly felt financially "unable" to liberate the human beings he had legal title to.[61] Following the emergence of the anti-Colonial movement for American independence and the accompanying wave of humanist ideology, Madison began voicing his disapproval of slavery. Like Jefferson and Washington, Madison indicated that he was searching for an alternative means of income that would allow him and his family to continue to enjoy a wealthy and privileged lifestyle.[62]

Madison contended that slavery was on the road to gradual extinction on its own. Left alone it would eventually die. The Founding Father pointed to the anti-slave-trade clauses in the U.S. Constitution that would formally end slave trade by 1808.

However, when the Constitution was drafted, Madison stood for the protection of the rights of slave owners to hold Africans as property.[63] Immediately prior to the Revolution, Madison displayed little sympathy toward black emancipation. In a letter written to William Bradford, Madison wrote of his fear that if violence broke out between the American colonists and Britain "an Insurrection among the slaves may & will be promoted." He wrote that blacks, "those unhappy wretches," had organized and chosen a leader in order to revolt when the British arrived. Madison contemptuously wrote, "they foolishly thought [it]would be very soon & that by revolting to them they should be rewarded with their freedom." He recommended steps to stop the spread of the insurrectionary mood and to crush those who were organized.[64]

Madison's apparent antislavery efforts peaked during the first session of the U.S. Congress, when he spoke in favor of the creation of a colony on the coast of Africa where former slaves would be settled. Expressing an idea that he would never relinquish, Madison argued the case for "free" black removal. Late in life, Madison continued to prove faithful to the slaveholder's cause by supporting the curious theory of "diffusion," which maintained that the expansion of slavery was the only way to ensure its eventual demise.[65] Throughout his life, Madison supported colonization of blacks outside of America. Like his friends Monroe and Jefferson, he felt that it would be impossible for free blacks to live with whites and shared the view—as did Benjamin Franklin until late in life—that America was best as a "white man's country."[66]

JAMES MONROE, GABRIEL, AND BLACK REVOLUTION

On August 30, 1800, a white Virginian of Henrico County learned that the enslaved Africans in the area were planning an armed revolt. The man promptly contacted the governor, James Monroe, who immediately called out the militia and stationed armed patrols at key installations in the area. This early warning, following weeks of rumors about a planned uprising along with an untimely thunderstorm, perhaps gave the authorities the time they needed to prevent the rebellion and take fearsome vengeance on the freedom-seeking Africans.

The leader of the African revolt, a blacksmith named Gabriel Prosser, was not only inspired divinely but also encouraged by the success of the Haitian revolution led by Toussaint L'Ouverture. Gabriel and his brother Martin had studied the Old Testament and sought lessons from the known Pan-African diaspora, or scattering of races. Gabriel was an early Pan-African nationalist who sought to capture territory for an African state on the North American continent. Preparing as extensively as he could, given the limitations on slave and non-slave black mobility in the Richmond of 1800, Gabriel tried to memorize the layout of the city by noting the key strategic installations during his trips within it. The other rebels included his brothers, Martin and Solomon, and his wife, Nanny. As Africans who burned with anger at the enslavement of their people, they eagerly awaited an opportunity to take a bold leap toward emancipating themselves and their brethren.[67]

Three columns of slave rebels were to march on the city and hit the strategic points. All white people were to be executed, with the exception of French, Quakers, and Methodists. The estimated number of Africans involved in the insurrectionary plans ranges from 20,000 to 50,000. It embraced people from several adjacent Virginia counties and many others in Richmond. The fear displayed by the whites during and following the rebellion was fully justified by the elaborate scope and impressive sophistication of the planned rising coming on the heels of the Haitian Revolution.

On the day of the revolt, despite the leaking of the plans, approximately 1,000 Africans made their way to the planned meeting place. Every conceivable homemade weapon was carried by the determined men and women, some of whom arrived on horseback. Only a few had guns; others had scythes, knives, and cruder weapons. Due to the detection of the plan and an unusually heavy thunderstorm that made a key bridge impassable, the revolt was postponed and the rebels dispersed. Governor and future president James Monroe led the bloody repressive effort. The African leader Gabriel was captured weeks later in Norfolk. During the time that Gabriel successfully eluded capture, whites themselves tasted some of the terror Africans had grown accustomed to. Nevertheless, during this repression, hundreds of Africans were taken into custody by the police and military forces, and eventually about 35 of them were hanged. Gabriel himself was put in chains, returned to Richmond, and quickly sentenced to hang.

At his trial, Gabriel was fully conscious of the historic importance of his failed effort at rebellion and held his head high, stating nobly:

> "*I have nothing more to offer, than what General Washington would have had to offer, had he been taken by the British and put to trial by them. I have adventured my life in endeavoring to obtain the liberty of my countrymen, and am a willing sacrifice to their cause. . . .*"[68]

Gabriel's captors went all out to force him to betray his fellow rebels and the African slave community. Gabriel wouldn't budge, remaining faithful to his sacred cause of African liberation and apparently realizing the importance of the example he would set in going to his death with dignity. Eventually, Governor James Monroe himself tried to get him to talk. Monroe's attempt was in vain as he reported that the rebel leader was determined to die without betraying his people. As Gabriel bravely went to the gallows, a newborn African infant, just five days old, struggled to adjust to his new surroundings on a slave plantation in nearby Southampton County. His name was Nat Turner.

During the years following the Gabriel-led revolt, James Monroe rose in national prominence, becoming the fifth president of the United States in 1817. Born in 1758 to a slaveholding family in Westmoreland County, Virginia, he moved to Williamsburg, the colonial capital, when he began college at age 16. In Williamsburg, Monroe was swept into the emerging anticolonial movement. Within a year, he had joined a group of men who carried out an attack on the Governor's Palace. Following independence, Monroe quickly began to assume prominent positions in the new nation. In 1782, he was elected to the House of Delegates in Virginia. By the turn of the century, Monroe had become the governor of Virginia.

After the extensive plans laid by enslaved Africans to seize their freedom were revealed, Monroe worked feverishly to ensure that future such actions would never occur. Uppermost in his memory were the recent events in Santo Domingo (now Haiti) that ended slavery there and culminated in the hasty flight of the slaveholders.[69] Governor Monroe himself was shaken by the scope of the planned slave revolt. To Thomas Jefferson, Monroe emphasized the seriousness of Gabriel's Revolt, "It is, unquestionably the most serious and formidable conspiracy we have ever known of the kind: tho' indeed to call it so is to give no idea of the thing itself." Governor Monroe maintained a strong military presence until the rebels were executed and no enslaved African military activity could be detected.[70] Monroe pardoned some, but 35 were executed.

The following years witnessed no letup in black attempts to gain liberty by arms. Nevertheless, many rumored plots were probably a product of the fear and guilt of whites in slave-populated areas. Plans for revolt and rumors of planned revolts occurred again in 1801 and 1802 in Virginia. In January 1802, an alleged slave-revolt plan rocked Nottaway County, Virginia. Governor Monroe, in speaking to the Virginia legislature, told members to expect continual revolts since the blacks were experiencing a growing hunger for freedom—a fact he attributed to the increase of "free" blacks in the area.[71] The subsequent trials surrounding the rumored slave-revolt plan spread panic among whites as waves of new "arrests" swept several Virginia counties. Monroe recognized that the "spirit of revolt has taken deep hold in the minds of the slaves."[72]

Weighing heavily on Monroe's mind was the recent success of the Haitian Revolution, which made black power in the Americas a harsh new political reality. The stream of news coming from Haiti fostered a new pride and assertiveness among blacks and harsher repression from whites. After the Gabriel-led revolt was crushed and the spate of executions of rebels and suspected rebels had sated the thirst of local whites for vengeance, a search began for alternatives to execution for slave rebels. Consideration was given to transporting the rebellious slaves to a region in the western part of the American continent. However, Jefferson and other leaders did not view it as a wise and prudent step to encourage the growth of a state of black former slaves in the West. Sierra Leone, Africa, was also considered, but finally an agreement was reached to keep the rebels in prison until they were sold to slave traders who agreed to sell them outside U.S. borders.[73]

THE MISSOURI COMPROMISE OF 1820

President James Monroe's role in securing the Missouri Compromise left no doubt about where his priorities lay. Scorning those who would scotch white unity for the antislavery cause, Monroe and former President James Madison supported the statehood of Missouri with no restrictions regarding slavery. As noted, Monroe, Madison, and Jefferson supported the "diffusion" theory, which held that the best way to aid blacks and end the repugnant institution of slavery was for the institution to spread as widely as possible. Jefferson expressed his support for the "diffusion" theory in an 1820 letter to Congressman John Holmes, asserting that slavery's expansion would lead to increased happiness and aid emancipatory efforts.[74] Marquis de Lafayette wrote Jefferson of his skepticism regarding the validity of the "diffusion" theory. Apparently viewing it as an elaborate justification for the perpetuation of the institution of slavery, Lafayette questioned Jefferson's logic. "Are you Sure, My dear Friend, that

France's Marquis de Lafayette questioned the American tradition of slavery.

Extending the principle of Slavery to the New Raised States is a Method to facilitate the Means of Getting Rid of it? I would Have thought that By Spreading the prejudices, Habits, and Calculations of planters over a larger Surface You Rather Encrease (*sic*) the difficulties of final liberation."[75]

The Missouri Compromise allowed for the simultaneous admission of Maine and Missouri to the Union and attempted a "final" settlement of the slavery controversy by providing for states north of the 36° 30° line to be admitted as "free" states and those south of it as slave states.[76] This landmark agreement forestalled the deep fissure in white unity that proved so bloody forty years later. Former president Thomas Jefferson, commenting on the Missouri Compromise, prophetically pointed to a North-South divide that "coinciding with a marked principle, moral and political, once conceived and held up to the angry passions of men, will never be obliterated; and every new irritation will mark it deeper and deeper." Jefferson despaired that this break in white national unity would ruin the revolutionary generation of 1776's accomplishments and was consoled only by the fact that he would not be alive to "weep over it."[77] Jefferson went on to advocate a "states' rights" position that brooked no federal interference with the institution of slavery.[78] In a letter to John Adams in January 1822, Jefferson spoke of his fear that black emancipation would result from Congress's power to intervene in the affairs of individual states. Alternately, he wondered aloud whether this would be "the tocsin of merely a servile war."[79] Jefferson, joined by South Carolina's John C. Calhoun, also favored seizing Cuba, in part to prevent it being "revolutionized by the negroes" in Adams's words.[80] Later, the Jefferson mantra on "states' rights" was taken up by Calhoun.[81]

CHAPTER TWO

AMERICAN PRESIDENTS AND THE BATTLE TO CONSOLIDATE SLAVERY, 1824–1861

THE ANTISLAVERY OF JOHN QUINCY ADAMS

In 1824, John Quincy Adams, a Federalist, benefited from a presidential contest in which the pro-slavery forces split their votes among three candidates: Andrew Jackson, William Crawford, and Henry Clay. The election went to the House of Representatives, where, finally, John Quincy Adams emerged as the sixth president-elect of the United States. The administration of John Quincy Adams marked a temporary break in the consecutive slave-owning American presidents just as his father, John Adams, had interrupted the string of Virginian slave-owning presidents. And just as his father had barely squeaked into office, so did the younger Adams. However, it is notable that both of the Adams's "antislavery" sentiments had very little impact on their policies with regard to Africans and slavery during their administrations.

In the case of President John Quincy Adams—a minority president—such timid moves as proposing that two delegates attend the Panama Congress, a summit of newly independent

John Quincy Adams had antislavery views, but he did little to help the African-American people.

South American nations, were anathema to the slaveholder-dominated American political elite. Adams recommended viewing the Panama meeting as a forum for the development of "the more effectual abolition of the African slave trade."[1] This was squelched, however, by the fear on the part of powerful Southern politicians of any conference that might consider the abolition of slavery in any nation. For three full months in 1825, the Jacksonian opponents of Adams hammered away at the specter of the United States attending a conference where abolition of slavery and the slave trade would be discussed. Such discussions raised in their minds the horrible specter of Haiti or "new" Haitis, which sent them into a frenzy. Adams's opponents, including the next president Andrew Jackson himself, seized upon these issues to play the "race" card against him.[2] Rebuffed on these limited antislavery thrusts, Adams, duly chastened, failed to initiate any further moves challenging the "Slave Power" for the remainder of his one-term presidency.[3]

Prior to his presidency, John Quincy Adams played an active role in national affairs. In 1804, Adams sided with the South in opposing amendments that would restrict slavery in the Louisiana territory.[4] Later, despite his reputation for opposing slavery, while he served as President Monroe's secretary of state, Adams clearly gave higher priority to his white American national unity than to his desire to eliminate slavery. Adams reflected the sensitivity of the American establishment to British violations of their international rights, making cooperation with the British to eliminate the slave trade difficult to achieve. Despite the consensus that the slave trade could not be stopped without routine searches of ships off the coast of Africa, Secretary of State John Q. Adams dropped his opposition to the continuation of slavery, refusing to sacrifice any American sea rights. The British minister asked him at one point if there were any greater moral evil than the trade in slaves. Adams replied, "Yes, admitting the right of search by foreign officers of our vessels upon the seas in time of peace: for that would be making slaves of ourselves." Adams complained that the British were pressuring the Americans excessively to help end the slave trade.[5]

THE DENMARK VESEY REBELLION, JOHN QUINCY ADAMS, AND BLACK SEAMEN

In July 1822, the uncovering of a massive conspiracy among African slaves in and around Charleston, South Carolina shook the slave society's foundations. Denmark Vesey, the leader of the revolt, was himself free of enslavement and could not bear to see his fellow Africans, including his own children, subject to the arbitrary whims of their slave masters.[6] He held a fervent belief in equality using both secular and religious logic in arguing for black liberation.[7] Hundreds of homemade weapons were manufactured, detailed plans for the capture of the arsenal were laid, and other preparations made for the armed revolt. However, this elaborate and extensive plot was betrayed, leading to the arrest of 131 Africans in Charleston. Ultimately, 37 were hanged, most heeding Peter Poyas who advised, "Die silent, as you shall see me do."[8]

In the aftermath of the Vesey slave rebellion, legislation was passed to further restrict the African ability to carry on international, national, regional, or local political communication. The free movement of black sailors, from either foreign countries or North, was targeted as potentially "incendiary." The new law required that they be confined to jails while their ships were in port. Knowledge of the emancipation of Africans in the British colonial holdings in the Caribbean was spread via this source, as well as a more detailed understanding of events in Haiti and elsewhere. One segment of opinion posits a direct connection between blacks in Santo Domingo and the rebellion led by Denmark Vesey. Monday Gell, another leader of the revolt, revealed the Santo Domingo connection by the use of the black seamen. Hence, the South Carolina establishment mandated the imprisonment of all black sailors while their ships were docked in the port of Charleston.[9]

Secretary of State John Quincy Adams felt that the law violated the rights of black citizens from the North and certain international treaties.[10] Adams lodged a subsequent protest with the South Carolina governor, which was soon supported by a U.S. Supreme Court decision. This pressure on the South Carolina elite was ultimately unsuccessful as they refused to rescind this law.[11] Later, the Carolina Senate declared that their "duty to guard against insubordination or insurrection," was "paramount to all laws, all treaties, all constitutions."[12] This "nullification," an extreme version of "states' rights" doctrine, succeeded since the northern forces had no heart for a drawn-out fight on the question. The jailing of black seamen continued.[13]

Adams's position during the "Nullification Crisis" was that the conflict among slaveowners confused the real conflict at issue. At this early point in American political history, Adams foresaw the dangerous division among whites. The real question to Adams was "whether a population spread over an immense territory, consisting of one great division of all freemen, and another of masters and slaves, could exist permanently together as members of one community or not; that, to go a step further back, the question at issue was slavery.[14]

CONGRESSMAN JOHN QUINCY ADAMS AND THE GAG RULE

John Quincy Adams seemed to have been more antislavery both before and after his four-year term as president. In late December 1835, northern abolitionists began using the tactic of submitting petitions for abolition of slavery to Congress. Having been recently aroused to action by the issue of abolitionist tracts in the southern post offices, southern congressmen charged that these petitions would incite nearby slaves in Washington, D.C., Maryland, and Virginia to armed revolt. In early 1836, John C. Calhoun, then a powerful South Carolina senator, said that the Senate must protect southern senators from such insults that implied that slaveholders were sinners and that such remarks must be prohibited in the Senate.[15] Calhoun felt that discussing the abolition issue at all, raised the prospect of giving courage to the "free" blacks in the North who sought to liberate their brethren by force of arms.[16] He warned that abolition might occur and that blacks would then inevitably enslave the whites.[17] Far from considering any emancipation decree, however gradual, Calhoun championed

Senator John C. Calhoun was an avid supporter of slavery.

the institution of slavery, seeking its expansion into the southwest, Mexico, Cuba, and beyond.

In May 1836, Congressman Henry Laurens Pinckney of South Carolina introduced a resolution that would table "all petitions, memorials, resolutions, propositions, or papers, relating in any way, or to any extent whatsoever, to the subject of slavery or the abolition of slavery. . . ." The resolution stipulated that "no further action whatever shall" be taken on the measures.[18] The slave owners and their supporters realized that merely to even begin to consider the subject of black freedom and the abolition of slavery posed great dangers for the stability of the slave system. Any knowledge that there was hope, or a slim opportunity to achieve black emancipation, was liable to inspire revolutionary slave movements. By necessity, white rights were also substantially restricted, thus the "Gag Rule" effectively impaired freedom of speech for American citizens.

For eight long years, Adams waged a lonely battle in the House of Representatives against the "Gag Rule." Each session of Congress would renew the rule, forbidding the right of citizens to petition Congress on issues involving slavery. In the two years of 1837 and 1838, almost 200,000 petitions against slavery and 32,000 against the "Gag Rule" itself were received in the House, but not one was heard.

In the House, Adams prophetically warned against the consequences of America's expansionism:

Mr. Chairman, are you ready for all these wars? A Mexican War? A war with Great Britain, if not with France? A general Indian war? A servile war? And, as an inevitable consequence of them all, a civil war? . . . From the instant that your slaveholding states become the theatre of war, civil, servile, or foreign, from that instant the war powers of Congress extend to interference with the institution of slavery in every way by which it can be interfered with.[19]

THE PRESIDENCY OF
ANDREW JACKSON

In 1828, Andrew Jackson won the presidency with John C. Calhoun as his vice-presidential running mate, defeating the incumbent President John Quincy Adams. By 1833, Calhoun and Jackson were locking horns over the issue of "nullification." Without the right to nullify, a South Carolina–centered sector of the southern slaveholding elite argued that the only remedy would be to secede from the Union. By 1833, with Jackson's key intervention, nullification was defeated, a victory he felt was key to the defense of slavery. Pointing to the growing threats to American unity posed by Calhoun and others, Jackson contended that they overestimated the extent of abolitionist sentiment in the North, thereby exaggerating the threat to slavery. The forestalling of a wider split during the nullification crisis of 1833 postponed the day of reckoning that eventually would occur some thirty years later.[20] During mid-summer 1835, a new threat to national unity emerged. Abolitionists had flooded South Carolina's postal system with antislavery messages to South Carolinians, thereby striking at the heart of the antebellum totalitarian system where freedom of the press did not exist.

One of the many antislavery cartoons created by William Lloyd Garrison, editor of the Liberator.

These messages were viewed as insurrectionary despite their appeal to white humanitarian sentiment. Still reeling from the 1831 Nat Turner revolt only three years before, slaveholders again pinned the blame upon abolitionists such as William Lloyd Garrison, editor of the *Liberator*. Almost immediately the plantation elite encouraged mob action to seize the abolitionist appeals and burn them in huge bonfires in Charleston.

President Jackson fully sympathized with this sentiment and, rather than insisting that "free" citizens have the right to consider pleas to their conscience, he asked that the postmaster hold them and keep a list of the names of the white citizens who would incite the blacks to rebellion.[21] Any suggestion that Africans be emancipated was viewed by the president as tantamount to treason.

Andrew Jackson was born in 1767 in South Carolina during a period in which the Catawba Indians were being removed from their land. At the age of thirteen, he served in the Revolutionary War.[22] Orphaned early in life, he moved to Charleston and became solicitor by the age of twenty-two. The next year, he achieved the position of U.S. attorney, and by thirty he was a U.S. senator. Yet the personality and outlook of Andrew Jackson emerged within the context of a violent era and setting. Not only was the future president implicated in massacres of Native Americans, but when nudged, he would slay white men also. A May 1806 duel with Charles Dickinson, who dared to argue with Jackson after a horse race, escalated after Jackson beat a youthful friend of Dickinson's with a cane. Dickinson, an expert gunman, felt obliged as a "gentleman" to challenge Jackson to a duel. Jackson allowed the expert shot to shoot first and was wounded. Then he allowed his rival, who had exhausted his ammunition, to suffer before he fatally shot him.[23]

Following his rapid rise to prominence, Jackson acquired a great deal of the land made available by the expropriation of the indigenous population. By 1795, it is estimated that Jackson and his business partner owned approximately 25,000 acres (10,100 ha). Soon the newly wealthy Jackson began to formulate plans to open a general store in Nashville. However, before the store could open its doors to customers, a swirl of financial instability took place, resulting in Jackson's loss of much of his ill-acquired fortune. In order to return to solvency, Jackson sold his estate, "Hunter's Hill," and many Africans, and moved to a smaller plantation only 1 square mile (2.6 square kilometers) in area. He also sold many of the enslaved Africans he owned.

Later, this plantation was developed extensively and eventually gained fame as the Hermitage.[24]

Jackson finally opened his dream store. This thriving enterprise sold a wide variety of commodities, most notably African slaves. They were literally sold down the river to Natchez or New Orleans for Jackson's profit.[25] In conducting his business affairs, Jackson was infuriated by any restrictions on his slave-trading and slave-owning "rights." The United States agent to the Choctaws, Silas Dinsmore, was charged with arresting every slave traveling with a white man if he could not produce a certificate proving his ownership. Many slave owners were irritated by this and complained in Nashville to Jackson. As a slave trader Jackson had a direct concern since he sent slaves south to be sold. Jackson had occasion to travel to Natchez and had to pass through Dinsmore's post when he returned. Determined to teach Dinsmore a lesson, Jackson gave his enslaved Africans rifles and, brandishing one himself, passed through the post without a certificate with Dinsmore mysteriously gone.[26] When he reached Nashville, Jackson remained determined to oust Dinsmore from his post. He wrote G. W. Campbell, a Tennessee congressman, asking has "it come to this? Are we freemen, or are we slaves? Is this real or is it a dream?" asked Jackson, a man whose ownership of African "chattel" slaves peaked at 150.[27]

"Old Hickory's" role in the 1814 Battle of New Orleans won him the title of the "Hero of New Orleans." Jackson enthusiastically reversed a policy that prohibited the participation of "colored" or "men of color" from the military defense of the city. When the Louisiana governor suggested to Jackson that black men be enlisted, he received an enthusiastic reply:

Our country has been invaded and threatened with destruction. She wants soldiers to fight her battles. The free men of color in your city are inured to the Southern climate and would make excellent soldiers. They will not remain quiet spectators. . . . They must be either for, or against, us. Distrust them and you make them your enemies, place confidence in them, and you engage them by every dear and honorable tie to the interest of the country, who extends to them equal rights and privileges with white men. . . . [28]

Despite the fact that the commissioned officers were white, the local Louisiana whites opposed the arming of free blacks whom they regarded as disloyal and a threat to slavery's security. Jackson persevered in his policy, however, extending to the black volunteers 160 acres (65 ha) of land and $124 in payment for their service. Jackson's move was clearly borne of military necessity, and speaks less to his liberalism than it does to the increased power of blacks in America during periods of crisis, especially wartime.[29]

During this period, a strategic fort was seized in Northern Florida by 300 African maroons accompanied by thirty Native American allies. The stronghold, on the Apalachicola River, was stocked with 3,000 muskets, carbines, and pistols, 763 barrels of gunpowder, and 300 kegs of rifle powder. It was seized from a group of Seminoles, who were given the fort by the British, courting their support in the war against the United States. In short order the "Negro fort" became a beacon for African slaves seeking freedom. It constituted a direct threat to the maintenance of slavery in the area, and was perceived as such by the area's white population. Raids and other aggressive actions by blacks took place from the stronghold. The African fort in Florida became a base for forays against nearby slave plantations.

General Andrew Jackson was happy to receive a directive to eliminate this source of black resistance. After obtaining assurances from the Spanish Governor of Pensacola that he would allow the American troops to destroy the Apalachicola River fort, they attacked and besieged it for ten days. The U.S. troops were frustrated in their effort to flush out the African maroons until they scored a direct hit on an ammunition dump. The explosion took 270 of the Africans' lives, and the fort was retaken. Only 40 Africans survived. Their leader "Garcon" was hanged, with his captors citing his treatment of Americans, which included burning and tarring a white man captured on the river.[30]

BLACK RESISTANCE IN
JACKSONIAN AMERICA

The periodic crises involving blacks fleeing from slavery proved detrimental to the maintenance of national unity in the long run. The fear of individual and mass flight from slavery had been a major concern of slave masters since the early days of the colonies. The New England Articles of Confederation of 1643 included a clause providing for the return of escaped slaves.[31] By the American Revolution a fugitive slave clause guaranteeing the return of fugitive slaves was hammered into the United States Constitution. Later two federal Fugitive Slave laws were enacted.[32] During the years following 1776, the chances of successful escape changed with the evolving demography and economy of slavery. During the earliest years escape was facilitated by the proximity of Native American populations. Indeed, the haste with which Native American communities were eliminated was due, in part, to the desire to secure slaves within a virtually inescapable environment. During the Jacksonian era, the lack of development of many areas allowed maroon communities to grow. The diminishing prospects for escapes to maroon colonies coincided with enhanced opportunities for escape to northern urban areas. As the decades passed, black communities in the northern cities grew and slaves in the border slave states began to flee to these refuges.

An estimated 30,000 blacks escaped slavery prior to the Civil War.[33] The black willingness to push the boundaries of the American social system to its limits was reflected by the increasing number of blacks taking flight from enslavement. These Africans included the famed Harriet Tubman, who repeatedly returned to the hell of slavery to rescue some 300 people. She could boast that she "never lost a single passenger"[34] on her Underground Railroad. Thousands fled from enslavement, collectively serving to heighten the sectional tensions among whites. By the 1850s, the issue of fugitive slaves would prove to be a volatile one, fateful for the destiny of the nation.

While antislavery sentiment grew slowly among whites in the North, black militancy developed at a faster pace there. Vig-

Harriet Tubman (far left) and a group of former slaves whom she helped to freedom

ilance committees were organized to protect black fugitives from slave oppression. There were many instances in which force was used to rid the black community of slave catchers. In the years 1801, 1826, and 1828, there are recorded instances of Africans in New York City beating back slave catchers. These and countless other unrecorded instances served to solidify Africans as a people, imbuing these half-free communities with a sense of their own power, and altering the way they perceived the world. Increasingly, blacks sought and were able to organize and emancipate themselves to defend their interests against those of their sworn enemies. Of particular concern to the emergent urban centers of black power were the activities of the American Colonization Society, which sought to rid the nation of "free" blacks by setting up African colonies. These budding centers of black power posed a distinct threat to the perpetuation of slavery and were perceived as such by slaveholders. The fears of the American Colonization Society were justified by the pivotal roles played by "free" Africans in the fomenting of slave rebellions, including the 1822 Charleston revolt led by Denmark Vesey.

The northern white population, sharing many of the racial views of their southern counterparts, generally had little concern about the daily misery endured by millions of enslaved Africans. By consensus, northern political leaders agreed that the slave master had a right to pursue and seize his property. However, among whites, a slowly growing but distinctly minority sentiment opposed the entrance of slave catchers into northern communities. The day-to-day activities within the growing black communities in the North, and the black slave communities in the South, combined to exert a constant pressure upon the "Slave Power." Their efforts dovetailed with those of the slowing developing abolitionist movement among white northerners.

Abolitionism came to denote a form of "extremism," in effect, by the early American establishment. It was outside the bounds of respectability and legitimacy, such was the entrenchment of anti-black sentiment within the political culture of the early white American establishment. To dare to speak of black emancipation was taboo, and such an act would harm the career of any aspiring politician. In this manner, words and phrases denoting African freedom or black liberty were effectively banned from the political discourse of American life during the mid-1800s. Succeeding years saw this prohibition maintain itself, albeit in new forms. Every president until Hayes, and many following him, condemned abolitionism and abolitionists in no uncertain terms. Other forms of "antislavery" sentiment among whites spoke in vague terms of a gradual withering away of slavery. During the 1830s, any "antislavery" ideas accepted within the confines of mainstream American political thought necessarily had to repudiate abolitionism and give its blessing to the positive side of the system of slavery. These were the boundaries of established American political thought and behavior within which presidents from Jackson to Lincoln adhered.

THE PRESIDENCY OF MARTIN VAN BUREN

Martin Van Buren was born in 1782 in the small Dutch village of Kinderhook, New York. Although he came from a family with a history of slaveholding and he owned at least one slave himself at the late age of forty-two, Martin Van Buren professed to be antislavery from his youth.[35] His father, Abraham Van Buren, a farmer, innkeeper, and local politician, owned six Africans as slaves. His own ownership included an African named "Tom," who was fortunate enough to eventually escape. After ten years, he was located by a white in a nearby town who offered to purchase him. Van Buren sold him for fifty dollars, stipulating that he be "taken without violence."[36] Van Buren's mild antislavery views acted merely to detour his early political career. Martin Van Buren once wrote to a prominent Richmond, Virginia, editor and asserted that through the mechanisms of the national political parties the slavery issue could be kept a non-issue.[37] Following his rise to national prominence, Van Buren opportunely dropped his antislavery positions. Despite the fact that his political opponents would often ridicule his former lukewarm antislavery stance, as the heir of Andrew Jackson, Van Buren inherited the baton of leadership of a young Democratic Party dedicated to the preservation of slavery. Van Buren attempted to quiet Southern fears that he would tamper with slavery by assuring slave owners that even if the North was so inclined, the Constitution prohibited any inference with slavery. He promised that, as president, he would vigorously act to protect their rights, including their rights to hold and exploit Africans in any manner that they wished.[38]

HARRISON AND TYLER: VIRGINIAN SLAVE-OWNING PRESIDENTS

In November 1840, William Henry Harrison was elected president of the United States. The general, famed as "Old Tippecanoe," won the presidency as a Whig with John Tyler, a slave-owning Democrat, as his vice president. Harrison lasted only one month in office, dying on April 4, 1841. His death was attributed to overexposure, and—despite being treated with the state-of-the-art of the era's medicine, which included being leeched and bled—he succumbed to pneumonia.[39]

Harrison was born in 1773 on Berkeley Hundred, a Virginian Tidewater plantation in Charles City County. He was the son of Benjamin Harrison, one of the signers of the Declaration of Independence and the governor of Virginia. After relocating to Indiana, Harrison rose to national prominence. Following his attainment of the status of a leading presidential candidate, he immediately sought to squelch rumors that he had once been an abolitionist.[40] He reassured the South that slavery would be safe under a future Harrison administration. He was able to point to a congressional record of pro-slavery actions, such as voting to lift the ban on slavery imposed by the Northwest Ordinance.[41]

Shortly after reaffirming his antipathy for abolitionism and settling in at the White House, Harrison died. Fellow Virginia native John Tyler took office amid much concern. Tyler hailed from Charles City County, Virginia, the same county that Harrison was raised in, and similarly had deep roots among the slave-owning elite of the Colonial period.[42] He was born in 1790 on the Greenway, a 2,500-acre (1,010 ha) plantation that held forty enslaved Africans. Born to John and Mary Armistead Tyler, Tyler experienced a childhood that resembled those of Jefferson and the other slave-owning Virginian presidents.[43] Attacking abolitionists vigorously, Tyler was a vigilant defender of the system that gave him prominence from birth. Oddly, despite his self-proclaimed weak stomach at the very sight of slave markets, it made him "physically ill," he remained constantly in search of slaves to purchase.[44]

During the mid-1830s, Tyler expressed confidence in the self-perceived kinder and gentler methods of exploiting his black slaves. "I trust that all will go on smoothly in harvest," he wrote. "My plan is to encourage my hands, and they work better under it than from fear. The harvest is the black man's jubilee."[45] Tyler argued that slavery represented both an improved quality of labor and productivity in comparison to the use of free white laborers, whom he termed "lazy."[46]

Following Nat Turner's rebellion in 1831, and the subsequent crisis surrounding the southern post offices, Tyler began to suspect that the "black man's harvest" might involve more than mere crops. By 1835, John Tyler's anger at abolitionists boiled over as he blamed them for inciting Africans to rebellion:

Nat Turner (left) being caught by an angry slave owner

The unexpected evil is now upon us; it has invaded our firesides, and under our own roofs is sharpening the dagger for midnight assassination, and exciting cruelty and bloodshed. . . .[47]

Tyler focused his outrage on abolitionists who had turned the "post-office department" into a "vehicle for distributing incendiary pamphlets," aiming to "despoil us of our property at the hazard of all and every consequence."[48] Tyler complained that slave owners were "represented as demons in the shape of men," while abolitionists such as Garrison were portrayed as "philanthropists—the only lovers of the human race—the only legitimate defenders of the religion of Christ." The abolitionists "patted" the "greasy little fellows on their cheeks" and gave "them most lovely kisses," Tyler complained.[49]

JAMES POLK, ZACHARY TAYLOR, AND THE EXPANSION OF SLAVERY

Born in 1795, James Knox Polk grew up in a politicized family that stressed independence from the central government.[50] As a young attorney, he was soon elected to Congress, serving there for fourteen years. Working closely with his mentor, Andrew Jackson, Polk gradually rose to prominence on the national political scene. The eventual owner of a slave plantation in Mississippi, Polk would play key roles in the Gag Rule battle, the effort to maintain white unity around black enslavement, and the successful mid-nineteenth-century expansionism of America.

Polk's initial speech in the House of Representatives set the tone for his entire career. In it he expressed his regret that the "unfortunate subject" of slavery had entered the national debate indirectly through the discussion of related issues. Polk quietly conceded in the manner of the Founding Fathers that slavery was an evil, but an evil which had been foisted on white Americans by the British, their oppressors.[51] As the speaker of the House, Polk was in a key position during the period in which petitions to end slavery began to be increasingly lodged. Polk was wary of the threat of black slave rebellion and felt that it was foolish to carry on any dialogue concerning abolition of slavery because blacks might take notice. Speaking in Tennessee's plantation belt, Polk criticized "the incendiary and intermeddling ethers of the Abolition Convention lately held in London," stating that he feared quoting from the proceedings because the passages were "too dangerous to be made known to the numerous slaves within hearing."[52] Polk, on another occasion, termed abolitionism "fanatical, wicked and dangerous agitation" on a "delicate question."[53]

By 1844, Polk's efforts to defend slavery won him the Democratic nomination for the presidency. As president, Polk led the efforts to expand the border of the United States. The term "Manifest Destiny" was coined during the 1840s by John L. Sullivan, a prominent editor. During this time, American expansionism foresaw the removal of non-white indigenous inhabitants from Texas westward. Slave owners sought fresh lands for expansion, having exhausted much of the land of the Southeast.[54] The indebted status of Mexico to the United States presented Polk with the rationale for conquest of the huge chunk of the nation's territory.

"Old Rough and Ready" General Zachary Taylor, was another in the string of slaveholding American presidents during the antebellum era. Born into a slave-owning family, his father's ownership of Africans increased from seven in 1790 to thirty-seven in 1810.[55] Zachary Taylor's leadership of military actions against Native American communities accompanied his growing land and slave holdings. In 1822, Taylor became the commanding officer at a post in Baton Rouge, Louisiana, and purchased a plantation nearby. In 1830, Africans enslaved on his Louisiana plantation died in droves due to overwork and brutality.[56] By the late 1840s, he could claim 145 human beings as property.[57] Taylor's Mississippi cotton plantation had 127 enslaved blacks on it at the time of his death in 1850. During his campaign for the presidency, opponents charged that Taylor had a total of 300 enslaved Africans, a charge the presidential candidate denied.[58]

The campaign of 1848 that pitted Taylor against Democrat Lewis Cass was marked by a silence on the subject of slavery by the two leading presidential candidates.[59] The Whig Taylor was known to be a defender of the South and slave-owner interests. The Democratic Party platform opposed any federal interference in slavery. Taylor and his running mate, Millard Fillmore, defeated the Democratic ticket to win the 1848 presidential election.

President Zachary Taylor, however, died five days after consuming an excessive amount of cherries and milk on the Fourth of July 1850. Vice President Millard Fillmore assumed office in mid-July 1850.

MILLARD FILLMORE AND BLACK RESISTANCE TO SLAVERY

After Taylor's death in mid-1850 and Fillmore's accession to the presidency, the new president was pressed to vigorously enforce the Fugitive Slave Act, a feature of the Compromise of 1850. In October 1850, Fillmore was asked to authorize the use of federal troops to seize an escaped African slave from locals who were helping him. While Fillmore complied with this request, his larger problem was that these incidents were becoming commonplace; in February 1851 in Boston residents of the local black community rescued an enslaved fugitive, Frederick "Shadrack" Wilkins, from a courtroom.[60] He was successfully transported to Canada following this. Each such event heightened tensions and strained the threads of national unity among whites, often reverberating within the halls of Congress itself.[61]

For his part, Fillmore complied with the slavemasters' wishes in vigorously pursuing Africans who escaped from slavery.[62] His primary objective was to avoid a splitting of the Union, and in this effort Fillmore was willing to concede key points to the slaveholders. His support of the Fugitive Slave Act allowed him to gain valuable southern political support. Despite this, the unfolding events seemed to undermine his goals. Late in Fillmore's presidency, in March 1852, the publication of Harriet Beecher Stowe's *Uncle Tom's Cabin* served to further polarize northern and southern whites.[63] Fillmore's last message to Congress displayed his fear of both the disintegration of national unity and of black vengeance. Fillmore predicted a bloody Haitian-like revolution in America if blacks were not expelled.[64]

PRESIDENTS PIERCE AND BUCHANAN IN DEFENSE OF SLAVERY

Although New Hampshire's Franklin Pierce was from a Northern state, his position on slavery and abolition was clear.[65] In his inaugural address, President Pierce stated his belief that "involuntary servitude" is constitutional and "stands like any other admitted right."[66] Fulfilling a campaign pledge, President Franklin Pierce vigorously enforced the Fugitive Slave Act. In 1854, after Anthony Burns, who had escaped from slavery in Virginia, was recaptured in Boston, there was a popular outcry against his return to slavery. In response, Pierce hastily dispatched a ship to transport the captive back to Virginia, earning him the label of "the chief slave catcher of the United States."[67]

James Buchanan was born in 1791 in rural Cove Gap, Lancaster County, Pennsylvania. In 1826, Buchanan declared slavery to be "a great political and moral evil" but voiced his great fear of the prospect of free blacks. Echoing a theme common to the slaveholding Colonial elite, Buchanan blamed Britain for American slavery. Buchanan was nominated by the Democratic Party, as it was felt that he could win against the newly formed Republican Party.[68]

As the pro-slavery President-elect James Buchanan took the inaugural oath on a Holy Bible, the Supreme Court was in the middle of deliberations over the Dred Scott case. President-elect Buchanan wrote to Supreme Court Justice James Grier urging a decision that would halt the agitation to abolish the institution. Thus, bending the Constitution, Buchanan seems to have influenced the eventual decision of the Court that declared that no black, "slave or free," was or was able to be a United States citizen.[69] Two days after Buchanan's inauguration, the Dred Scott decision was rendered by the U.S. Supreme Court. This historic decision declared that the Constitution's due process clause prohibited any action to interfere with property in any state including human property. Thereafter, no United States legislative body could constitutionally bar slavery from any place in the nation. As for Africans, they had no rights "which the white man was bound to respect."[70]

Dred Scott was the subject of great debate during the Buchanan administration.

THE DISINTEGRATION OF NATIONAL UNITY

There were many events that marked the nadir of American unity. The remarkable attack on Senator Charles Sumner, an antislavery senator from Massachusetts infuriated northern opinion. Following Sumner's criticism of Senator Andrew F. Butler of South Carolina, Sumner was writing at his desk in the Senate chamber when he was approached by Butler's nephew, Congressman Preston S. Brooks, also of South Carolina. Angrily shouting at Sumner, Brooks began to brutally beat him with his cane, severely injuring Sumner. To northerners this ugly incident further alienated them from the South, hardening the view of the South as tyrannical and undemocratic.

In late 1857, after Buchanan had settled in at the White House, a crisis involving Kansas broke out. Despite the abundant evidence of fraud in a vote for slavery—and that the vast majority of white settlers in Kansas rejected slavery—President Buchanan accepted the result. In early 1858, he asked Congress to make Kansas a pro-slavery state.[71] Amid a rapidly deteriorating federal Union, President Buchanan delivered his fourth State of the Union message, lamenting that a quarter of a century of agitation had filled the minds of slaves with foolish notions of liberty which undermined the "sense of security" "around the family altar."[72]

The last sessions of Congress prior to Lincoln's inaugural and the outbreak of Civil War were tense affairs. Soon another ominous sign of white national dissolution appeared: The Democratic Party was inactive as a national organization in April 1860. The party, which traditionally had united whites around slavery and served as a wider franchise for white males for three decades, split into southern and northern sections. Now, for the first time in American political history there were no truly national political parties.

These events dramatized, electrified, and widened the gulf between whites of the North and whites of the South. In the truncated world view of the slave-owning South, events from Nat Turner's revolt through the emergence of abolitionism to the increase in African urban resistance were all linked together to a general northern conspiracy to betray them to the enslaved Africans. The Southerners exaggerated the threat to slavery posed by the Republicans and Lincoln and were driven to irrationality by their very rational fear of black rebellion. They sought to insulate their captives, both physically and mentally, with the aim of breaking the human spirit. To achieve and maintain this, only a "peculiar" set of political and economic institutions would suffice. The achievement of southern social stability was an impossibility where no semblance of free speech, free press, and freedom of assembly existed. The Gag Rule, the postal system crisis of 1835, and the question of slavery's expansion all involved the perceived and real necessity of the South to attempt to seal off the brutal system from outside observers, from outside news, from communications with those outside the system. Increasingly, protected from contaminating outside influences, the South fell victim to its self-perpetuating mythology.

Black unity was at a historic high point culturally with many of the previous ethnic and regional differences having been erased during the long years of slavery. Communication networks among Africans had developed to a high level of sophistication despite the repression of the slave system. Many individuals dreamed constantly of any opportunity to realize both their own individual freedom and their people's freedom. This opportunity was soon to come.

CHAPTER THREE

THE CIVIL WAR AND THE CHALLENGE OF BLACK EMANCIPATION, 1861–1900

THE CIVIL WAR, ABRAHAM LINCOLN, AND BLACK EMANCIPATION

On April 12, 1861, Fort Sumter, South Carolina was attacked by southern forces marking the beginning of the U.S. Civil War. The war raged for almost four solid years, until the formal surrender of Confederate forces at Appomattox Courthouse in Virginia on April 9, 1865. After Lincoln was inaugurated as president he attempted again to head off secession by reassuring southern leaders that there was no "reasonable cause for such apprehension. . . ."[1] Promising to "deliver up" escaped Africans to their southern captors while stressing the need for American unity, Lincoln said, "I am loath to close [for] We are not enemies, but friends."[2]

Many Africans in America rejoiced at this historic rupture of national white unity. Like thousands of others, Abby Kelley Foster, a long-time abolitionist, exclaimed "Glory to God."[3] From the onset of the conflict, Frederick Douglass stressed the necessity of emancipating blacks from slavery and enlisting them in the fight against the Confederacy. He prophetically asserted that the "Negro is the key of the situation—the pivot upon which the whole rebellion turns."[4]

Particularly disheartening to blacks was Lincoln's reversal of a limited emancipation proclamation by General Fremont that allowed the return of escaped slaves to their captors in the South.[5] Gradually, events forced Lincoln to endorse measures against the South that threatened ownership of property in human beings. On August 6, 1861, Lincoln signed the Confiscation Act, which emancipated the slaves of those Confederates waging war against the North.[6] However, after General David

Frederick Douglass devoted his life to fighting the institution of slavery.

Hunter proclaimed slaves of Georgia, South Carolina, and Florida free, Lincoln denounced him declaring his proclamation "null and void."

During a meeting on August 14, 1862, at the White House, President Lincoln spoke to five hand-picked black leaders and blamed the war on both the existence of slavery and the presence of blacks. Lincoln told the delegation that funds had been appropriated for colonizing blacks in regions such as West Africa.[7] The national black community was dead set against such colonization schemes. In April 1862, at a large meeting in Boston, it was resolved that when blacks in the United States desired to leave the country, they would determine the time and method of financing the move themselves. Until that moment, they vowed to resist fiercely any attempt to force them out of the country.[8]

After he learned that Lincoln was still advocating black colonization outside of the United States, Douglass was outraged.[9] Lincoln's view that the "problem" of blacks was thrust upon white Americans by their British oppressors translated into a viewpoint that blacks themselves were the source of the problem. For this reason, Lincoln sought to remove the black presence from the United States. Douglass responded that, "A horse thief pleading that the existence of the horse is the apology for his theft or a highway man contending that the money in the traveler's pocket is the sole first cause of his robbery are about as much entitled to respect as is the President's reasoning at this point. . . . No, Mr. President, it is not the innocent horse that makes the horse thief, nor the Negro that causes the foul and unnatural war. . . ."[10]

The preliminary Emancipation Proclamation of September 1862 posed the possibility of both a compensated emancipation and the emigration of blacks from the country. The issuing of the final Emancipation Proclamation of January 1, 1863 was made by military necessity. The increasingly desperate northern military situation, marked by plummeting white morale, forced Lincoln to declared the slaves free in order to undermine the economic, and therefore military, basis of the South.[11]

The newly decreed Emancipation Proclamation was quite vulnerable in its first months as any serious Union military setback threatened it. One scenario Lincoln considered involved the partial withdrawal of black emancipation and the restoration of slavery. Lincoln told Douglass that within this scenario, all of the blacks who remained enslaved would not be emancipated, only those who had fled from slavery and the South would be allowed to remain free. Douglass was undoubtedly dismayed by the sudden possibility of reversing an emancipation that many had already celebrated.[12]

In July 1863, Douglass visited President Abraham Lincoln at the White House.[13] Douglass could not avoid being emotional about the enormity of his personal odyssey. "No man who had not worn the yoke of bondage and been scourged and driven beyond the beneficent range of the brotherhood of man by popular prejudice [could] understand the tumult of feeling with which I entered the White House."[14] President Lincoln dispensed with a formal introduction of Douglass, telling the famed abolitionist, "Mr. Douglass, I know you; I have read about you, and Mr. Seward has told me much about you." Lincoln had heard of one of Douglass' eloquent speeches in which his policy had been described as "tardy" and "vacillating." Lincoln denied any vacillation but said, in essence, that he was slow, but sure. He stated that once he adopted a position he never backed away from it.[15] Douglass, an agent of the government charged with the recruitment of black soldiers, presented the case for equal treatment in pay and rights for blacks in the military. Lincoln refused to grant equal pay immediately, pointing to the prevailing white prejudice, but promised that the pay would eventually be equalized. At this point, Douglass described Lincoln as wholly free "from popular prejudice against the colored people," remarking that he "was the first great man that I talked with in the United States freely, who in no single instance reminded me of the difference between himself and myself, of the difference in color. . . ."[16]

During early 1864, Douglass was critical of Lincoln's plans for the formerly enslaved Africans. Lincoln did not foresee enfranchising blacks in the South as voters and was amenable to a liberal plan of reintegrating southern whites into the political system. Since Lincoln had not sought black emancipation but rather black emigration, it was not surprising that Lincoln foresaw continued white supremacy and a social system closely resembling slavery in the post-war South.

THE EARLY BACKGROUND
OF ABRAHAM LINCOLN

In February 1809, Abraham Lincoln was born in a Kentucky log cabin to Thomas Lincoln and Nancy Hanks. Following his appointment as the postmaster in New Salem, Illinois, Lincoln studied law and launched his political career by becoming a candidate for a seat in the Illinois legislature. Early on, Lincoln decided that it was to his advantage to take political positions that were within the limits of acceptability of the period's racial views. His first opportunity to vote in favor of black rights involved the expansion of the franchise in Illinois to include blacks. Lincoln took this opportunity to vote "no" during this 1835–1836 session of the legislature.[17] By the age 28, however, Lincoln had officially registered his opposition to slavery in the Illinois House of Representatives, but he also felt obliged to frame his "antislavery" position by stressing a twin hostility toward abolitionism—commonly used as a convenient scapegoat by aspiring politicians.

Yet, Lincoln did evince an unusual degree of empathy with black murder victims of white mobs. In an 1837 speech, Lincoln lashed out at an "increasing disregard for law which pervades the country," specifically targeting "savage mobs" that had perpetrated "outrages." Blacks accused of conspiring to rise up were hanged, Lincoln noted. Following these actions, white men thought to have sympathized with the blacks were treated likewise. Lincoln deplored this perceived trend toward mob rule.[18] Later, in this speech he criticized the chaining and burning to death of a "mulatto" in St. Louis who, according to Lincoln, was murdered "within a single hour from the time he had been a freeman attending to his business and at peace with the world." However, he later reversed himself and asserted that the African "forfeited his life by perpetration of an outrageous murder upon one of the most worthy and respectable citizens of the city, and had he not died as he did, he must have died by the sentence of the law in a very short time afterward." Lincoln was careful to not show any sympathy with this individual African, "As to him alone, it was as well the way it was as it could otherwise have been. . . ."[19]

Abraham Lincoln was elected to the U.S. Congress under the banner of the Whig Party in August 1846. Lincoln was a practical border-state politician who remained within the boundaries of what would win and keep him in office. In Congress, Lincoln often sided with the slave owners and vacillated on the issue of the slave markets within the district. Lincoln's and other politicians' interest in getting rid of the large slave markets in the shadow of the Capitol stemmed from their profound embarrassment before the growing number of foreign visitors and diplomats. The sight of coffles of Africans chained and on auction blocks tended to undermine the national image of freedom and democracy.[20]

In 1849, Lincoln announced his intention to introduce a bill to abolish slavery in the District of Columbia. He proposed a gradual emancipation decree that would pay slave masters for their loss of "property." Despite the inclusion of a provision that would deliver fugitive blacks back to slavery, Lincoln was immediately faced with the slaveholders' political backlash. The powerful political and economic interests that protected slavery in Washington exploded with fury upon learning of the proposed legislation. John C. Calhoun, the powerful South Carolina senator, a life-long foe of African emancipation, led the opposition. Calhoun, as always, warned that if blacks were given a morsel of liberty, they would revolt and enslave the white race. Lincoln, realizing that the end to his political career loomed imminent, never introduced the bill.[21]

At the end of the June 1858 Republican State Convention in Springfield, Illinois, Lincoln delivered his "House Divided" speech. Declaring that "A House Divided Against Itself Cannot Stand," Lincoln expressed his doubt that the nation could last "permanently half slave and half free." He foresaw not disunion but rather a severe national crisis after which the nation would again be united.[22]

During his 1858 debate with Stephen Douglas, Lincoln denied seeking any "social equality between the white and the black races," asserting that there was "a physical difference between the two" that would "forever forbid" any equality between them. This being the case, Lincoln was "in favor of the race to which I belong." Thus, in essence, he asserted that white supremacy does not necessitate robbing the blacks of the fruits of their labor.[23]

A speech by Lincoln in 1858 stressed that the Founding Fathers "desired that slavery should be put in course of ultimate extinction. . . ."[24] Lincoln sought to affirm his fundamental opposition to slavery, in responding to charges by his arch-rival Stephen Douglas and other political foes that he favored slavery's ultimate demise. Lincoln, however, also sought to reassure slave owners, declaring that "there is no right and ought to be no inclination in the people of the free States to enter into the slave States and interfere" with the institution of black enslavement.[25] Lincoln's "states' rights" position was quite a quite convenient shield to deflect questions of the morality of slavery's existence.

Abraham Lincoln speaking with an African-American family on the White House lawn

ABRAHAM LINCOLN: "PREEMINENTLY THE WHITE MAN'S PRESIDENT"

In April 1876, Frederick Douglass delivered a speech in Washington, D.C., on the occasion of the unveiling of the Freedmen's Monument in Memory of Abraham Lincoln.[26] Douglass asserted that in Lincoln's "interests in his associations, in his habits of thought, and in his prejudices, he was a white man." Douglass stressed that he was "preeminently the white man's President, entirely devoted to the welfare of the white man."[27]

He criticized Lincoln for his readiness to "deny, postpone, and sacrifice the rights of humanity in the colored people to promote the welfare of the white people of this country. . . ." Douglass noted that "To protect, defend, and perpetuate slavery in the states where it existed Abraham Lincoln was not less ready than any other President to draw the sword of the nation. . . ."[28] Blacks were "not the special objects of his consideration," he told the audience. Addressing the whites who were present, he said, "You are the children of Abraham Lincoln. We are at best only his step-children; children by adoption. . . ."[29]

Douglass stated that African-Americans never relinquished their hope that Lincoln would act in the interests of humanity:

Our faith in him was often taxed and strained to the uttermost, but it never failed . . . when he strangely told us that we were the cause of the war; when he still more strangely told us that we were to leave the land in which we were born; when he refused to employ our arms in defence of the Union; when, after accepting our services as colored soldiers, he refused to retaliate our murder and torture as colored prisoners; when he told us he would save the Union if he could with slavery . . . when we saw all this, and more, we were at times grieved, stunned, and greatly bewildered; but our hearts believed while they ached and bled. . . .[30]

AFRICAN-AMERICANS: MAKING EMANCIPATION A FAIT ACCOMPLI

A black convention in 1865 resolved to demand the right to vote, citing the fact of black participation in the armed forces of the nation. The delegates also vowed to push for the acquisition of property, education, and to expand the number of black teachers.[31] The mood of black delegates was definitely upbeat although the assessments of the black condition were frank.

William D. Forten's speech recognized that African-Americans just emerging from slavery were a "deeply injured" people. He voiced his contempt for whites who maintained that America was "a white man's country" following the Civil War when "it required the strong arm of over 200,000 black men to save it." The key question, Forten eloquently maintained, was how blacks would respond to the crisis looming before them during the post–Civil War period.[32]

Africans won emancipation from slavery, but at a horrific price in human terms. Altogether some 180,000 black soldiers participated in the Civil War. Some 37,000 perished in the war, amounting to roughly one-fifth of those enlisted. During the entire war, black soldiers participated in 499 military engagements and 39 major battles.[33] African non-combatants played a key role in the winning of emancipation also. The mass stoppage of work on the white male-depleted southern plantations, the fleeing to Union army lines, the sabotage of work, the espionage, the political organizing in the northern black communities, and black political leadership all successfully converted the Civil War into a battle for the emancipation of blacks. The Emancipation Proclamation merely put an official stamp of approval on what was already quickly becoming reality. By the middle of the Civil War, there would be no return to the days of slavery; Africans, taking advantage of white disunity, imposed their will upon the situation.

New forms of oppression would rise to ensnare African-Americans within their grip, but the classic slave system was dead and gone. There was no time to celebrate slavery's death, for new challenges to their dearly won freedom awaited them. Emancipation fundamentally changed the nature of relations between blacks and U.S. presidents. Soon, blacks won legal political representation but faced new obstacles to their advance, circumscribing their economic, social, and political liberties.

Former slaves making their way off the plantations following the issue of the Emancipation Proclamation

ANDREW JOHNSON AND THE RECONSTRUCTION OF BLACK OPPRESSION

Fate was unkind to African-Americans when the assassin John Wilkes Booth struck down President Abraham Lincoln. His successor, Andrew Johnson, was a determined anti-African racist whose politics sharply veered from those of Lincoln. Precious years in the brief historical window of opportunity for social, political, and economic advances were lost by the coming of Johnson to the presidency.

The softness of white northern support for black political rights was quite evident. In repeated electoral tests among the white voters of the North, referenda on black voting rights were narrowly defeated in state elections.[34] Few could support such radical measures as those proposed by Congressman Thaddeus Stevens, which would have given 40 acres (16 ha) of land to every adult African-American freed by the Emancipation Proclamation. This measure would have given the newly freed slaves an opportunity to achieve economic self-sufficiency and independence from the rule of the old slave masters. Yet, in the atmosphere of 1866 and 1867, some of the most favorable years for the attainment of black rights, this was politically improbable due to the prevailing racial prejudices among whites in both the North and South. Instead, new relationships arose from the conflict between the effort of African-Americans to carve out and construct new lives for themselves and that of resistant whites determined to take advantage of the black community. It was a busy period in which African-Americans attempted to reorganize their lives in every way in light of their new freedom. Perhaps the most important item of business for individuals and families emerging from slavery was to move physically from the old plantation. Some black preachers, following emancipation, advised blacks first to move away from the land of the old slave masters and seize their freedom assertively.[35] Often the former slave masters immediately resorted to force, trying to keep black individuals and families from leaving the plantation and generally gaining the cooperation of the authorities in this effort.[36] In other cases, the newly emancipated people refused to leave the plantation, adamantly insisting that they deserved part of the land by virtue of the centuries they and their ancestors had labored on it.[37] The preferred new arrangement by blacks was tenancy, as opposed to wage working, and renting land, rather than sharecropping, since these arrangements ideally allowed for autonomy, a fuller family development, and the possibility of eventual land ownership.

PRESIDENT ANDREW JOHNSON: A CONFEDERATE IN THE WHITE HOUSE.

After taking office as president and finding "stout" Negroes at work on the White House grounds, President Andrew Johnson immediately inquired as to whether white men had been replaced by these blacks.[38] Johnson openly stated his view that whites, and whites alone, should govern the South. Following his selection as Lincoln's running mate in June 1864, Johnson regarded the Civil War as part of a battle against the "slave aristocracy" by men who represented the common man. Johnson indicated that he supported slavery's abolition because it destroyed "an odious and dangerous aristocracy." According to Johnson, in his home state of Tennessee more whites than blacks were freed by the Emancipation Proclamation.[39]

In a June 1864 speech, Johnson expressed his horror at being charged with favoring black-white equality.[40] Later, Johnson offered to be the "Moses" of the emancipated Africans. He stated, "humble and unworthy as I am, if no better shall be found, I will indeed be your Moses, and lead you through the Red Sea of war and bondage to a fairer future of liberty and peace...."[41] As W. E. B. DuBois

Andrew Johnson held the view that blacks would never be equal to whites.

pointed out, these are the remarks of a man who had said more than once in reference to black equality: "Damn the Negroes."[42]

Johnson was born in a two-room shanty in Raleigh, North Carolina in 1808. His father died early, forcing young Andrew to rely on taking apprenticeships, which seriously compromised his personal freedom.[43] Johnson eventually settled in Greenville, Tennessee, marrying Eliza McArdle in 1827. His business as a tailor was successful, and he invested his excess income in real estate. Early in Johnson's political career, he voted in favor of a law that forbade non-enslaved blacks to own grocery stores, bars, or other types of enterprises.[44] Johnson resented enslaved Africans throughout his life as he felt their "alliance" with the master made them trample over the poor whites. But following his rise up the social hierarchy, Johnson acquired property in human beings. By the Civil War, Johnson held five black people as slaves, and once as many as eight Africans at one time.[45] During his early political career, he viewed slavery as a fundamental principle of American political life. Andrew Johnson felt that a measure that would give blacks the vote would:

> place every splay-footed, bandy-shanked, hump-backed, thick-lipped, flat-nosed, wooly-headed, ebon-colored negro in the country upon an equality with the poor white man.[46]

Johnson's political career took off after his 1845 victory in a campaign for a seat in the U.S. House of Representatives. Later, as a congressman, styling himself as the representative of the "common" white man, he assailed the "upstart, swelled headed, iron heeled, bobtailed aristocracy."[47] During the 36th Congress, Johnson said that if the effort to emancipate blacks was successfully accomplished, then whites, slaveholders and non-slaveholders alike would unite to exterminate the former slaves.

Johnson committed himself to personally participating in the genocidal effort.[48]

While President Johnson indulged the southern elite by liberally granting pardons to former Confederates, he acted to maintain the complete political disfranchisement of African-Americans, leaving them at the mercy of their former masters. Early in his administration, President Johnson directed the federal government to oust blacks from lands they had gained during Lincoln's term.[49] Johnson suggested that after "the tumult of emotions" died down, blacks would "receive the kindliest" treatment from "some of those on whom they have heretofore most closely depended," namely the former slave masters.[50]

The hallmark of Radical Republican politics during this era was the advocacy of black suffrage, and there was widespread support expressed at Republican gatherings across the nation for granting the vote to African-Americans.[51] Immediately following the assassination of Lincoln and Johnson's accession to the presidency, Senator Charles Sumner and others began pressing the new president to grant blacks the right to vote.[52] In particular, Senator Sumner diligently sought meetings with Johnson during the spring of 1865, imploring him to agree to black suffrage. Early on, Johnson seemed agreeable to the demand, leading the Radical Republicans to believe that he supported the African-American franchise. By 1865, however, Johnson maintained that the federal government had no role in fostering black suffrage in the former Confederate states. Johnson felt that his political position against black suffrage was politically safe, partly due to the outcome of a referendum among whites of the District of Columbia on black voting rights: District of Columbia whites resoundingly rejected, by the vote of 7,369 to 36, the black right to vote.[53]

In May 1865, Johnson told an audience of African-Americans that they would have to get rid of this "idea among them that they have nothing to do but to fall back upon the government for support in order that they may be taken care of in idleness and debauchery." Later that fall, he told an audience of black veterans that "Freedom is not simply the principle to live in idleness." Johnson's advice included moral strictures such as the need to avoid places of vice and ill-repute. Despite Johnson's moral advice to African-Americans, he himself created a quite a controversy when he slurred his way through his vice-presidential inauguration speech in a drunken semi-stupor.[54]

PRESIDENT JOHNSON'S MEETING WITH FREDERICK DOUGLASS

On February 7, 1866, a delegation, deriving from the Convention of Colored Men, met with President Andrew Johnson at the White House. Douglass and George T. Downing delivered statements to Johnson to begin the meeting. Both men implored the president to grant the vote to blacks as a matter of both justice and salvation for the newly freed African-Americans. Douglass told Johnson that, as president, he had "the power to save or destroy us, to bless or blast us."[55]

In his reply, Johnson stated unashamedly that he had bought and owned slaves. He explained that he took it as a point of honor, as did so many other slaveholders, that he had never sold a slave. He was devoted to his slaves to such an extent, Johnson declared, that he was actually the slave of them. All of his life's work had been risked for his slaves, he said. Johnson then began "blasting" the delegation for their apparent sins of lack of proper deference to a white superior. The president said that he didn't like to "be arraigned by some who can get up handsomely-rounded periods and deal in rhetoric, and talk about abstract ideas of liberty, who never periled life, liberty or property."

President Johnson turned to Douglass and said that poor whites and blacks had always been adversaries in a manner that implied that they always would be.[56] The black voter, Johnson asserted, would be in the control of the former slave owners who would determine how the former slaves would vote. Douglass disagreed, contending that they would vote together with the poor whites.[57] Johnson insisted that the black vote would lead to a race war, the result of which could, in his view, only end in the complete annihilation of African-Americans.

At one point during Johnson's long monologue, Douglass interrupted the president, which further irritated him. Johnson reminded Douglass that the Civil War was not fought with the goal of freeing blacks from slavery, rather this outcome was incidental to it.[58] While slaves were free following the war, in Johnson's view, the poor white man came out of it with nothing.

Douglass told the president "you enfranchise your enemies and disfranchise your friends."[59] Douglass spoke at length, contending that any such racial war could be averted by granting the right to vote to blacks. Johnson then declared that blacks should consider emigrating to another country. Douglass shot back that this would be impractical and quite unlikely given the lack of freedom of movement that accompanied the continued oppression and often slavery-like conditions blacks were subjected to. The former slave owners, moreover, were desperate for labor. The two leaders continued to exchange remarks as they departed.

The fallout from the confrontation was not long in coming. Immediately afterward, President Johnson spewed out a stream of negative comments about Douglass. He said after the meeting to a *New York World* reporter that the "damned sons of bitches thought they had me in a trap! I know that damned Douglass; he's just like any nigger, and he would sooner cut a white man's throat than not."[60]

The delegation of African-Americans also issued a statement following the meeting with the president. The statement dissected Johnson's justifications for black disenfranchisement and stated that any hostility between poor whites and blacks was "entirely reciprocal" and explained by the divide-and-conquer tactics used by slave masters.[61] The men noted that the poor whites were the "slavecatchers, slavedrivers, and overseers" who committed many crimes against Africans during slavery. Now, however, that slavery was gone forever there was no "cause of antagonism." If such an hostility exists as Johnson alleges, they maintained, then it would be even more unjust to "disarm the black man politically," noting that

Experience proves that those are oftenest abused who can be abused with the greatest impunity. Men are whipped oftenest who are whipped easiest. Peace between races is not to be secured by degrading one race and exalting another, by giving power to one race and withholding it from another....[62]

In spite of his confrontation with Douglass, President Johnson recommended appointing him to head the Freedmen's Bureau—a move designed to shore himself up politically. Sensing this motive, Douglass turned the offer down, viewing it as a move that would allow Johnson to deny he was acting consistently in the interests of the former slave masters. This turn of events moved one newspaper to comment, "The greatest black man in the nation did not become a tool of the meanest white."[63]

Following this incident, President Johnson vetoed the Civil Rights Bill, engendering such a backlash that it led to the first overturning of a presidential veto in the history of the United States.[64] The fissure between the president and the Republican

Party widened considerably after these events. Other events, however, electrified the atmosphere of this period. In Memphis, in May 1866, a massacre of African-Americans took place, resulting in 46 slain and some 75 wounded.[65] Later, in July 1866, in New Orleans, the Unionist Constitution Convention met in order to map a strategy to enfranchise blacks and disfranchise former Confederates. The overwhelmingly black group of delegates was attacked by a heavily armed mob of former Confederates. The police joined the attackers while the army was mysteriously away from the scene. Thirty-eight delegates to the convention were slain and many more wounded.[66] Johnson did not intervene on behalf of black civil rights, but rather he said that federal troops were a humiliation that white southerners need not be subjected to. [67]

Equally serious for any prospect of an improvement in the overall quality of black life was the passage of a series of laws designed to control black liberty. Apprenticeship laws were used to force the separation of black children from their families and ensure that they work as de facto slaves, generally for their former slave owners.[68] Deprived of the rights to hunt and fish, to graze livestock, and partake in other important activities, blacks found their economic opportunities to be severely restricted. Taxes were used as an instrument to coerce blacks back into arduous plantation labor. Vagrancy laws were similarly used to supply the former slave masters with unwilling laborers.[69] In addition, the legal segregation of public facilities was expanded to restrict black social rights. The increasing alienation of Johnson from Congress led to the events that culminated in his impeachment by the House of Representatives. Having run into conflict with Congress, the crisis peaked following Johnson's sacking of Secretary of War Edwin M. Stanton, in spite of Congressional objection.[70] Johnson was put on trial by the Senate and acquitted of the charge of "high crimes and misdemeanors."[71]

PRESIDENT ULYSSES GRANT AND THE END OF RECONSTRUCTION

President Grant continued Johnson's policy of leniency and sought the removal of the remaining restrictions on the political activity of former Confederates. Legislation to this effect was passed by Congress in May 1872.

Hiram Ulysses Grant was born in April 1822 in Point Pleasant, Ohio. The Civil War hero's career was slow in developing, despite his graduation from West Point and military experience in the war against Mexico.[72] Dogged by poverty as late as 1856 and 1857, only a few years prior to the war that would transform his life, Grant hauled and sold firewood at one point.[73] Grant utilized the slave labor of African-Americans, as many as twelve individuals, though he and his wife may have actually had legal title to only five.[74]

Early in the Civil War, Grant wrote his father expressing confidence in an eventual northern victory and the view that slavery would end following the war. Blaming blacks for the war, Grant predicted that "The nigger will never disturb this country again." Indeed, Grant viewed blacks as corrupting whites, and as inducing whites to commit immoral acts.[75]

Grant's reconstruction policies were partially designed to prevent African-American troops from upsetting the traditional racial social hier-

Ulysses S. Grant fought against the Confederacy, but he did not support equal rights for American blacks.

archy in the South. Grant and other national leaders believed that the presence of these troops would interfere with the labor and discipline of local African-Americans and politically undermine white rule. President Grant supported Freedmen's Bureau head General O.O. Howard's urging that the former slaves should place their faith in their old masters. Grant feared the effect of armed black soldiers on civilian blacks for what he said were "obvious" reasons.

The occupation of the South was mostly symbolic at that point. Only roughly 9,000 federal troops were stationed in the states of the former Confederacy, and Grant was reluctant to use them to protect black human rights. Despite rampant violence in 1871 against African-Americans in South Carolina, Grant made use of the new Ku Klux Klan enforcement law only once.[76] Nevertheless, Grant was reelected in 1872, due in large part to black voting power.[77] Northern business interests became warmer toward the former Confederate rebels, joining their denunciation of "carpetbaggers."

By 1874, only four states remained under Reconstruction governments: Louisiana, Mississippi, South Carolina, and Florida. In three important southern states—Mississippi, South Carolina, and Louisiana—black voters stood their ground until a wave of violence deprived them of their political rights. General John McEnery, a white Louisiana politician, vowed to "carry the next election if we have to ride saddle-deep in blood to do it."[78] In May 1874, 40 white leaders gathered in central New Orleans to plot their strategy to complete the "redeeming" of the remaining four states.

In July, the "White League" was formed clandestinely. In subsequent months, the organization spread throughout the South and increasingly used violence to drive African-Americans from leading political and economic positions and to eliminate any genuine black leadership. In 1874, in Vicksburg,

Mississippi, hundreds of blacks were slain as whites seized political power. South Carolina's Wade Hampton was clear on the method to be used in his state to eliminate black power. "Every Democrat," he declared, "must feel honor bound to control the vote of at least one Negro, by intimidation, purchase, keeping him away or as each individual may determine, how he may best accomplish it."[79]

This violence against African-Americans grew so serious that President Grant finally addressed the issue. He wrote the U.S. Senate in January of 1875, describing the Louisiana violence as "a butchery of citizens" that "in blood-thirstiness and barbarity is hardly surpassed by any acts of savage warfare. . . ."[80]

A deadlocked presidential contest in 1876 between Democrat Samuel Tilden and Republican Rutherford B. Hayes was all that was needed to set the stage for the full-scale abandonment of what national commitment to black civil rights remained.

RUTHERFORD B. HAYES AND THE COMPROMISE OF 1877

The deadlocked presidential election of November 1876 set the stage for the historic "Hayes-Tilden compromise." The electoral stalemate took place within the context of a Republican-controlled Senate and a Democratic-controlled House of Representatives. Democratic presidential candidate Samuel J. Tilden of New York conducted an openly racist campaign that stressed the need to bar African-Americans from the vote.[81] The quandary was resolved after Hayes promised to withdraw the remaining federal troops occupying Louisiana and South Carolina. Hayes would receive the support from the South that would enable him to become president. White southerners assured Hayes that they would not trample upon the rights of blacks and take advantage of the situation to repress their political opponents.

Rutherford B. Hayes, born in Delaware, Ohio, in 1822, became a brevet major-general in the Civil War and was wounded three times. By 1865, he was elected to Congress as a Republican. During his 1867 campaign for governor of Ohio, Hayes came down in favor of the franchise for African-Americans in Ohio and throughout the nation. Hayes was vehement in his rejection of the notion that the United States was a "white man's" country.[82] While Hayes narrowly won, the amendment for black voting rights failed by a large margin of 30,000.[83]

Following the forging of the "Gentlemen's Agreement" in 1877, Hayes couched his actions in terms of overcoming sectional and racial divisions. Voicing full confidence in white southerners, he eagerly believed their professions of goodwill toward blacks and ignored the grave predictions of a fierce repression of blacks after the pullout. Hayes's post-election "Goodwill Tour" was highlighted by an Atlanta speech in which he praised the unity in diversity exemplified by his audience and, then, turned toward the African-Americans in the audience to state: "I believe that your rights and interests would be safer if this great mass of intelligent white men were let alone by the general government."[84]

Soon conditions and despair among African-Americans deepened and led to acts of desperation such as the "Great Exodus" of 1878–1879, a long march out of the South to Kansas by African-Americans seeking to escape the oppression of the South.[85]

PRESIDENTS GARFIELD, ARTHUR, AND CLEVELAND: SYMPATHY FOR THE SOUTH

After Hayes decided not to seek reelection, James A. Garfield was nominated by the Republican Party as their presidential candidate. During the Civil War, Garfield supported the arming of Africans as soldiers, dismissing fears that this move might spark black slave insurrections. It would be bloody, Garfield responded, "but it is not in my heart to lay a feather's weight in the way of our black Americans if they choose to strike for what was always their own."[86]

After the Civil War, Garfield's position shifted farther in favor of black emancipation. Garfield's spirituality at the time influenced his view that the Civil War was God's retribution for the nation's sins of slavery. "For what else are we so fearfully scourged and defeated?" Garfield once asked.[87] Following the war, Garfield supported voting rights and introduced a resolution that would have ended the requirement that African-Americans in the District of Columbia carry passes.[88]

Soon, however, Garfield's progressive policies began to moderate. By 1870, Garfield heralded the "triumphant conclusion" of the fight against slavery with the passage of the 15th Amendment. This amendment gave blacks the right to vote. Now, Providence placed "upon the African Race the care of its own destiny. It places their fortune in their own hands."[89] Garfield came to advocate "states' rights" and maintained that the federal government was unable to respond to the wave of anti-black terrorism plaguing the South.[90]

Frederick Douglass and other black leaders suspected Garfield of anti-black sentiment. Their suspicions were well-founded. Although Garfield had backed black suffrage, he confided privately in 1865 that he had "a strong feeling of repugnance when I think of the negro (sic) being made our political equal and I would be glad if they could be colonized, sent to heaven, or got rid of in any decent way," lamenting that "colonization has proved a hopeless failure everywhere."[91] Garfield also once complained that Capitol Hill was too "infested with Negroes."[92]

The most striking fact of Garfield's presidency was its brevity. In July 1881, he was assassinated by Charles Guiteau in

Washington, D.C. On balance, the brief administration of President James A. Garfield merely continued the policy of fostering sectional unity initiated under Hayes.

President Garfield was succeeded by Chester A. Arthur. At that time, African-Americans began to seriously grapple with the persisting problem of the disregard the Republican Party held for their interests.

Born in Vermont in 1829, Chester A. Arthur rose to become an attorney in New York City. As president, Arthur continued the policies of his predecessors that ignored the systematic violation of African-American rights.[93] President Arthur's inaugural address justified the disfranchisement of African-Americans by the extent of illiteracy among the recently emancipated people.[94] These actions, and his lack of interest in enforcing civil rights laws, led to harsh African-American criticism of his administration.[95]

The 1884 election of Democrat Grover Cleveland ended the long string of Republican presidents in office since the Civil War. Not since James Buchanan won the presidency in 1856 had there been a Democrat in office. African-Americans overwhelmingly supported the Republican Party's nominee, James G. Blaine, who promised blacks "freedom and equality" and condemned violations of voting rights in the South.

T. Thomas Fortune, a contemporary African-American national leader, forecast disaster in the event of Cleveland's election. His editorial entitled "Colored Men Keep Cool," written in the aftermath of the Cleveland victory, reflected the unease blacks felt with the Democratic return to the White House.[96]

Following Cleveland's victory in the 1884 presidential election, there were unverified rumors that African-Americans in Washington, D.C., had targeted him for assassination.[97] During President Cleveland's 1888 reelection bid, the Democrats tried to present a racially liberal image to the black voter. Cleve-

President Grover Cleveland was elected in 1884 without black support.

land's acceptance letter included a "guarantee to our colored citizens" of civil rights and vague promises of aid.[98]

THE PRESIDENCY OF BENJAMIN HARRISON: DASHED HOPES FOR AFRICAN-AMERICANS

Sandwiched between the two administrations of Democrat Grover Cleveland was the administration of Benjamin Harrison, who was president from 1889 to 1893. Harrison, a prominent Republican lawyer-politician from Indiana, rose from a second lieutenant to a brevet brigadier general during the Civil War and

Benjamin Harrison agreed that African-Americans had been treated poorly in the South, but he refused to speak out against lynching.

gained some fame with General Sherman's campaign in Georgia.

As a U.S. senator, Harrison once commented, "We may place the U.S. Marshals at the polls, if we ever recover the Presidency. . . ."[99] In 1886, he felt that "the colored race in the South has been subjected to indignities, cruelties, outrages, and a repression of rights such as find no parallel in the history of civilization."[100] These were strong statements, words that if put into practice would have greatly relieved the political repression black communities felt throughout the South.

Only weeks prior to the 1888 Republican National Convention, Frederick Douglass delivered a stern warning to the Republican Party. African-Americans were increasingly conscious of being taken for granted by the Republican Party—partly as a result of the repugnance of the virulent anti-black racism of the Democratic Party. Douglass cautioned the Republican Party that "it [could] no longer repose on the history of its grand and magnificent achievements."[101] Now, it was necessary to halt the scourge of anti-black lynching across the nation.[102] Later, Douglass joined Mary Church Terrell in meeting with President Harrison to urge him in his annual message to Congress to make a statement against lynching. He refused to do so.[103]

Harrison was nominated on a platform that condemned the forcible disenfranchisement of African-Americans in the

South and called for federal action to protect black voting rights.[104] Harrison's words were greeted by African-Americans with a wary enthusiasm. During the three decades since emancipation, there had already been many broken promises from the Republican presidents they had been instrumental in electing.

With President Harrison's backing, the Lodge Federal Elections Bill, which would allow federal supervision of congressional races, was passed in the House by a vote of 155 to 149. It was labeled the "Force Bill" by resistant southern Democrats although no force was provided for.[105] However, after fierce debate the bill was ultimately defeated.[106]

GROVER CLEVELAND AND THE EMERGENCE OF BOOKER T. WASHINGTON

The second administration of President Grover Cleveland was quite similar to his first. At the 1892 Democratic Convention in Chicago, delegates hammered out a platform that opposed the Lodge Federal Elections Bill, contending that it would harm African-Americans even more than whites.[107] This was the key issue in Cleveland's campaign strategy of stoking white fears of black equality, termed "Negro domination." Cleveland took the position on the Lodge bill that it represented "a direct attack upon the spirit and theory of our Government."[108]

The edifice of Jim Crow laws, regulations, and customs were viewed by President Cleveland not as a problem but rather as a solution to the continuing problems stemming from the unplanned emancipation of African-Americans in the aftermath of the Civil War. While the watershed *Plessy v. Ferguson* U.S Supreme Court decision in 1896 was greeted with silence by Cleveland, there is little reason to suspect that he disagreed with its conclusion that upheld the legality of segregation in all spheres of life. Cleveland pointedly did not believe that African-

Booker T. Washington was an eloquent writer and educator.

Americans deserved equality—on economic, social, or political bases—with white Americans.[109]

Booker T. Washington's "Atlanta Exposition" speech, which called for a harmonious accommodation within a rigidly segregated system, was music to President Cleveland's ears. Cleveland wrote an approving letter to Washington a few days following his historic speech, saying, "Your words cannot fail to delight and encourage all who wish well for your race. . . ."[110]

It was the beginning of a new era. In 1895, Frederick Douglass—a wise old leader who had been tested and tempered by the heat of battles extending back to the early days of the abolition movement through the Civil War and into the post-Reconstruction Era—passed from the scene, active to the very last day of his life. The same year witnessed the emergence of a new leader, Booker T. Washington.

McKinley and the Era of the "White Man's Burden"

In 1865, William McKinley, Jr., was quite touched during a visit to a hospital packed with wounded Confederate soldiers. In fact, he was so moved by the emotional bonds with his estranged southern countrymen that he felt compelled to join the Masons, an organization that existed in both the North and South.[111] The warmth exuded toward the old adversaries of the South extended to his policies. As a critic of Radical Reconstruction, McKinley felt the South should be appeased.[112]

William McKinley, Jr., was born in 1843 in Niles, Ohio, into a family reported to have had an antislavery tradition. A Republican, McKinley was elected to Congress in 1876.[113] After becoming the governor of Ohio, McKinley continued to speak favorably of black rights. Within the Ohio Statehouse, the governor had criticized lynching and appointed blacks to some posts. But upon becoming a leading presidential candidate in 1896, McKinley reversed his views, and he no longer advocated positions at odds with the Southern political elite.[114]

The impact of McKinley's change of heart can be seen in his failure to respond to the Lake City, South Carolina, lynching of an African-American postmaster. Appointed by President McKinley, but abandoned by the McKinley administration and the federal government, the postmaster was forced to rely on his own resources to resist the threats and intimidation of white vigilantes. His home was eventually surrounded and set afire. While his wife and five other children escaped, the postmaster and one child were slain as they fled the burning home. President McKinley, elected with substantial African-American support, remained silent following this atrocity.[115]

With McKinley kneeling at the altar of sectional reconciliation, the structure of black oppression hardened in the South as social, economic, and political liberties were further restricted. Louisiana adopted a "Grandfather Clause," effectively disenfranchising tens of thousands of African-Americans while North Carolina used another method to disenfranchise blacks in that state. In 1898, in Wilmington, North Carolina, an antiblack riot left dozens dead, making clear the price of black activism during the McKinley era.[116] Senator "Pitchfork Ben" Tillman proudly recited his efforts to drive South Carolina African-Americans away from the political arena. "We have done our level best . . . we have scratched our heads to find out how we could eliminate the last one of them. We stuffed ballot boxes. We shot them. We are not ashamed of it."[117]

During the McKinley era, anti-black violence continued at a high level. Major riots occurred in the first decade of the 20th century in the cities of Springfield, Ohio; Springfield, Illinois; Greensburg, Indiana; Atlanta, Georgia; and Brownsville, Texas.[118] The early 1890s were the peak years of lynching, with 161 recorded lynchings of African-Americans in 1892.

Representative George H. White, the last African-American remaining in the House of Representatives, routinely witnessed a barrage of racist demagoguery and abuse during House of Representative sessions.[119] To his credit, during White's last term he introduced a bill to make lynching a federal crime. In Representative White's final speech to the soon-to-be all-white assembly, he declared:

> This, Mr. Chairman, is perhaps the Negroes' temporary farewell to the American Congress; but let me say, Phoenix-like he will rise up some day and come again. These parting words are in behalf of an outraged, heart-broken, bruised and bleeding, but God-fearing people, faithful, industrious, loyal, rising people—full of potential force.[120]

President William McKinley, Jr., was shot on September 6, 1901, by an anarchist.[121] He died eight days later. McKinley's heir was the energetic and ambitious Vice President Theodore Roosevelt. For once, it seemed, a stroke of good fortune would aid the African-American cause.

CHAPTER FOUR

AMERICAN PRESIDENTS FROM THE PROGRESSIVE ERA TO WORLD WAR II

THEODORE ROOSEVELT AND THE OUTRAGE OF BROWNSVILLE

On August 13, 1906, the wild shooting by an unknown group of men in the Texas town of Brownsville took the life of a bartender, while wounding a police officer who encountered the men. This ten minutes of random shooting into the street proved to be a pivotal element in the relationship between President Theodore Roosevelt and African-Americans.

The Brownsville events took place amid a period of racial tension in the Texas community. An African-American battalion that had been stationed in the town for only two weeks and two days had already been involved with three minor clashes with local whites who felt they were under "Negro domination." Following the shooting, the townspeople organized themselves into a "Citizen's Committee" and telegraphed President Roosevelt concerning their plight. Following a superficial investigation, President Roosevelt ordered another investigator to interrogate the twelve principal "suspects," directing him to find

African-Americans were sometimes disappointed by Theodore Roosevelt.

evidence proving their guilt. Roosevelt decided early on to dismiss the black troops en masse; however, he delayed his action until following the elections. His caution was fully justified since the African-American vote was important in his victory.[1]

The African-American community quickly protested that the Brownsville soldiers' rights to a fair hearing were violated. Prior to the affair, President Roosevelt had been thought of as a political ally of African-Americans.[2] However, following an independent investigation, it was suggested that it was impossible for the accused men to have been at the scene of the shooting since a routine roll call, which revealed that all men were accounted for, occurred simultaneous to the sounds of the firing of the guns.

Roosevelt vigorously defended his actions, terming the Brownsville violence an act "of horrible atrocity" and "unparalleled for infamy in the annals of the United States Army." He claimed that a "blacker crime never stained the annals of our Army."[3] The atmosphere grew angrier later, however, after Roosevelt endured criticism from a senator over the Brownsville discharges.[4] After Roosevelt had to be restrained from retaking the floor to respond to Senator Joseph B. Foraker's criticisms, he exclaimed, "some of the men were bloody butchers—they ought to be hung."[5]

Roosevelt's stance on Brownsville was consistent with his earlier speeches on the subject of black crime. On another occasion, Roosevelt warned blacks, "If colored men elect to stand by criminals of their own race because they are of their own race, they assuredly lay up for themselves the most dreadful day of reckoning."[6]

This was not Roosevelt's first experience with black soldiers. While Roosevelt once wrote that the black troops under his command in Cuba performed well, he disparagingly described the ability of the regular black troops in comparison to that of their white counterparts.[7] Roosevelt was adamant in his conviction that a white must serve as an officer to African-American troops. Once he recounted an incident illustrating what he viewed as the innate cowardice of African-Americans. Roosevelt reported that he "witnessed an extraordinary panic among the colored troopers," who were ordered to dig a trench. Roosevelt said that when he attempted to lead a march of the African-American troops back to the trenches

the rearmost men grew nervous, jumped forward and in a few seconds the whole body broke and came in like so many stampeded buffaloes, racing and jumping over the trench. . . .

Roosevelt continued to write that he "attributed the trouble to the superstition and fear of the darkey," who was only "a few generations removed from the wildest savagery."[8]

PRESIDENT THEODORE ROOSEVELT AND CIVIL RIGHTS

Theodore Roosevelt was born in the heart of New York City in October 1858. His family's paternal side traced its origin seven generations back to the mid-17th century on Manhattan Island. Early on, young Theodore was regaled with tales of life on the Georgia plantation where his mother grew up. Martha "Mittie" Bulloch Roosevelt was descended from a powerful slaveholding

Georgian family.[9] This background had a definite impact on Roosevelt's consciously white supremacist views. President Roosevelt confessed in 1904 that he had always felt that the passage of the 15th Amendment, giving blacks the right to vote, was a mistake.[10] Roosevelt charged his own party in the past with engaging in "hypocrisy" in its relationship with the whites of the South. For practically fifty years, in order to achieve black civil rights, Roosevelt asserted that the Republican Party had "encouraged" the "colored man in the south" to "antagonize the white man of the South."[11]

President Taft was more concerned with pleasing voters in the South than with giving African-Americans equal rights.

PRESIDENT WILLIAM HOWARD TAFT AND AFRICAN-AMERICANS

Secretary of War William Howard Taft won the 1908 presidential election over his closest challenger, Democrat William Jennings Bryan, by a comfortable margin. Through Taft, President Theodore Roosevelt's legacy lived on after he voluntarily relinquished his hold on the presidency. President William Howard Taft's inaugural address was marked by a promise not to offend the South by appointments that conflicted with their racial values. Taft continued the policy of his predecessors in declining to enforce the Constitution's 13th, 14th, and 15th Amendments.[12]

Through Taft, Roosevelt's alliance with Booker T. Washington remained intact. Philosophically, Taft and Washington shared, at least on the surface, common ideas about the African-American political, social, and economic role in the "New" South. Taft held that the "greatest hope that the Negro has, because he lives chiefly in the South, is the friendship and the sympathy of the white man with whom he lives in that neighborhood."[13]

PRESIDENT WOODROW WILSON AND SEGREGATION

In 1912, Bishop Alexander Walters, who had campaigned in 1908 for the Democratic candidate, lamented the extent to which the Republican Party had slid from the principles of Charles Sumner of the 1870s. Then head of the Colored Democratic League, Walters stated that "the dullest mind can see at a glance the difference between the [Republican] party as represented by Charles Sumner in 1870 and Theodore Roosevelt and William Howard Taft in 1912. . . ."[14] Walter's influence was instrumental in convincing W. E. B. DuBois to support Democrat Woodrow Wilson's candidacy and to spurn the Republicans Roosevelt and Taft. DuBois hinged his support for the candidate on the condition that Wilson make a statement supporting black civil rights. Wilson complied by issuing a remarkably mild statement.[15] In his bid for the White House, the former Princeton president failed to appear before any black audiences. Yet Wilson received more black support than was then usual for a Democratic presidential candidate, garnering an estimated five to seven percent of the black vote.[16]

Born December 28, 1856, in Staunton, Virginia, Thomas Woodrow Wilson grew up in an atmosphere steeped in anti-black sentiment. Wilson never developed beyond a sentimental attachment to the values and customs of his native region. Following an exclusive screening of D. W. Griffith's *Birth of a Nation*, Wilson approvingly termed the film, "History written in

Woodrow Wilson's White House was a segregated one.

lightning."[17] Throughout his career, he referred to blacks as an "ignorant and inferior race."[18]

Slavery, in Wilson's view, was of great benefit to Africans as it had led to more progress in America than had occurred in two millennia on the African continent.[19] In his *Division and Reunion*, he defended the slaveholders against "the charges of moral guilt for the establishment and perpetuation of slavery which the more extreme leaders of the antislavery party made against the slaveholders of the southern States."[20]

With President Wilson setting the example at the top, lower level federal bureaucrats took the initiative to step up efforts to segregate, exclude, and demote blacks.[21] In the Treasury Department and Post Office Department, separate toilets for blacks and whites appeared. Following the often chaotic transfer of black employees, by the summer of 1913, the only remaining

African-American male—out of a total of one thousand employees—worked with his desk surrounded by screens, to create the perception of separation.[22] In May 1914, a new requirement for those who applied through the Civil Service for government employment was put into effect: Photographs were used to visually discern the fitness of those applying.[23]

In November 1913, a delegation led by William Monroe Trotter presented a lengthy statement to Wilson. Trotter declared, "If separate toilets are provided for Latin, Teutonic, Celtic, Slavic, Semitic and Celtic Americans, then and only then would African-Americans be assigned to separation without insult and indignity."[24] Reflecting a confidence in the collective determination of African-Americans, the Harvard-educator editor warned the president of a massive "protest of African-Americans" from across the nation would "convince" him to alter course.[25]

President Wilson replied that he had been misrepresented and denied that "the spirit of discrimination" existed in his administration.[26] The president contended that the segregation order shown to him by the delegation was the first such "order of segregation" that he had seen.[27] While he promised delegates that the situation would be "worked out," segregation in the federal bureaucracy increased, which led to another meeting a year later.[28]

One year later, in November 1914, another African-American delegation led by Trotter met with President Wilson. The Boston editor presented the president with a detailed portrait of the segregation within the Treasury and Post Office Departments, describing several segregated restrooms, lunchrooms, dressing rooms, and workplaces. Trotter stressed that the "lavatory segregation is the most degrading, most insulting of all. Afro-American employees who use the regular public lavatories on the floors where they work are cautioned and then warned by superior officers against insubordination."[29] Trotter also indicated that black voters would punish Wilson at the polls for his actions.

President Wilson seemed irritated at Trotter's implicit threat declaring, "If the colored people made a mistake voting for me, they ought to correct it and vote against me...." President Wilson told the delegation, "it takes the world generations to outlive all its prejudices." His administration merely "did not want any white man made uncomfortable by anything that any colored man did, or a colored man made uncomfortable by anything that a white man did." Trotter declared that his delegation did not meet him as "wards" or "dependents" but rather were demanding the "vouchsafed equality of citizenship by the federal Constitution." President Wilson was angered by Trotter's tone and concluded that "if this organization wishes to approach me again, it must choose another spokesman."[30]

WARREN G. HARDING'S "OCTOBER SURPRISE"

Ohio kingmaker Mark Hanna once remarked, "I carry the Negro's vote around in my vest pocket."[31] African-Americans were not alone in realizing that they were traveling down a political dead-end street. Yet in 1921, the nation's ten million African-Americans greeted the Harding administration with relatively high hopes, following the eight years of retrenchment under Woodrow Wilson.[32]

Warren Gamaliel Harding was born November 1865 in the small village of Blooming Grove, Ohio. By 1882, Harding had graduated from small Ohio Central College in nearby Iberia.[33] Later, with two friends, he purchased the *Marion Star* for $300. Following Harding's victory in an election for the state senate in 1899, his political career skyrocketed. He was an unsuccessful Republican candidate for governor in 1910, but he was victorious in his race for the U.S. Senate four years later. Having established himself as a senator, Harding announced his candidacy for the president of the United States in December 1919. His real goal was to solidify his position for his reelection campaign to the Senate.[34] To his own shock, he won the Republican nomination.

Senator Harding's presidential campaign proceeded smoothly until an "October Surprise" almost derailed it. Suddenly, pamphlets appeared accusing Harding of having African blood, a damning accusation for a white American politician.[35] William E. Chancellor, an anti-black Wooster College professor, had researched Harding's background in Marion, Ohio. Harding, even in his childhood, was derided for having what his antagonists said was an African heritage. At the time of his marriage, his future father-in-law opposed the union, pointing to Harding's black blood. Harding almost had a physical altercation with him over the charge.[36]

Harding's ancestors migrated from Pennsylvania to Ohio and moved into a black community. They later moved to a white community; however, the impression that they were of African ancestry followed them. When young Warren would get into fights, he would invariably be called "nigger" and "coon."[37] Harding once said, "How do I know, Jim? One of my ancestors may have jumped the fence."[38]

While Senator Harding himself did not directly deny the charges, his campaign shifted into overdrive to counter the "smears." A Harding family tree was compiled by the Historical Society of Wyoming, Pennsylvania, and accompanied by a statement that his heritage consisted of "a blue-eyed stock from New England and Pennsylvania" of "the finest pioneer blood, Anglo-Saxon, German, Scotch-Irish, and Dutch." This "damage control" ultimately saved the campaign.[39]

Meanwhile, Harding, as a believer in black inferiority, narrowly avoided one of the emotional collapses that plagued him throughout his life. His wife too was reportedly "red-eyed from weeping" from the "vile" charge. The presidential candidate reportedly had to be restrained from roughing up Chancellor.[40] Finally, however, the storm blew over, and Harding's silence was rewarded as he won the election handily.

THE HARDING ADMINISTRATION AND AFRICAN-AMERICAN PROGRESS

Warren G. Harding was elected with overwhelmingly black support, and he became the first Republican in the White House in eight years. His election in November 1920 promised to speed the enactment of federal anti-lynching legislation, improve race relations, end the U.S. occupation of Haiti, and significantly increase African-American mid-level positions within the federal bureaucracy. The new president's inaugural address buoyed African-American hopes. The demand for action by the president and the Congress to end the scourge of lynching became a perennial feature of the black agenda presented to every president from Hayes to Truman. The response of each president to this demand was both a litmus test of their policies as well as a barometer of the level of national African-American political power. Harding declared that Congress "ought to wipe the stain of barbaric lynching from the banners of a free and orderly, representative democracy."[41]

The African-American enthusiasm for the new administration of President Harding was short-lived. It was soon apparent that fewer blacks than expected would be appointed to key positions; that no real White House push to enact an anti-lynching law would be made; that President Harding was gearing his politics to woo southern anti-black constituencies; and that no executive order desegregating the federal bureaucracy would be forthcoming. By October 1921, President Harding was in Birmingham, Alabama, speaking to a segregated audience of thousands of blacks and whites, warning African-Americans not to seek equality.[42]

PRESIDENT HARDING'S "SOUTHERN STRATEGY"

President Harding felt that the black presence in the Republican Party was hampering the efforts of Republican presidents to crack the solidly Democratic white South. This led many leaders of the party to desire the purging of the black presence within the party. Having long since abandoned the most progressive and liberal positions of the Reconstruction Era, Harding openly proclaimed his wish that African-Americans leave the Republican Party and join the Democratic Party.[43] In his Birmingham, Alabama, speech Harding said "both races" should be "uncompromisingly against every suggestion of social equality."

> *Indeed, it would be helpful to have that word 'equality' eliminated from this consideration; to have it accepted on both sides that this is not a question of social equality, but a question of recognizing a fundamental, eternal and inescapable difference.[44]*

Harding further stressed that recognition of these "eternal and inescapable" differences was key to future progress.

With an eye on his "Southern Strategy," Harding emphasized, that "racial amalgamation there cannot be," arguing against a nonexistent African-American demand. In the view of some sectors of the African-American community, President Harding was not against miscegenation, or mixed marriages, at all. "What they intend to say is that miscegenation should take place in a certain way. . . . Any amount of amalgamation is agreeable to these gentlemen, provided it comes by way of white men and colored women. Just guard the white woman from the Negro man! is what they desire to state."[45]

While he stated his commitment to "equal educational opportunity" for both races, he stressed that this did "not mean that both would become equally educated within a generation, or two generations, or ten generations." Assuring whites of the South that his view of racial progress for African-Americans did not involve any prospect of "social equality" in the foreseeable future, Harding viewed black education as a way of creating leaders with the proper, subservient outlook. He deplored the development of "group" organizations among blacks, contending that blacks should remain powerless and place their faith in the benevolence of southern whites. Harding said,

I may be dreaming, but it seems to me that the colored man of the South has his only opportunity by falling in the ranks behind the leadership of white men, until such a time as he may be able to control the Legislature. I may be wrong in this, but I am determined, live or die, sink or swim, to adhere to this policy.[46]

President Harding, who had a history of depression, became enfeebled, ill, and confused by early 1923, and he died in office of a heart ailment in August 1923.

PRESIDENT CALVIN COOLIDGE: STRONG WORDS, WEAK ACTIONS

President Calvin Coolidge took office upon the death of President Harding. The Coolidge administration did little to improve African-American prospects for social, political and economic progress.

Born on July 4, 1872, Coolidge continued the Harding policy of ignoring black interests and placating the South. The prosperous Coolidge years were marked by a continuation of the status quo in the South with respect to black civil rights. As did his predecessor, President Coolidge hid behind the doctrine of "states' rights," avoiding his obligation to enforce the Constitution.

In December 1927, Coolidge declared, "History does not anywhere record so much progress made in the same length of time as that which has been accomplished by the Negro race in the United States since the Emancipation Proclamation. . . ."[47] In June 1923, speaking at Howard University, Coolidge described black progress "on this continent" as "one of the marvels of modern history." Clearly, Coolidge's conclusions were premised on a view that Africans were and remained backward and inferior. To President Coolidge, the conversion to Christianity during the bondage of slavery apparently justified the centuries of black enslavement.[48]

Calvin Coolidge believed that his administration had improved the lives of black Americans.

The overall impact of the Coolidge administration forced a more widespread realization among African-Americans that they were prisoners of a two-party system, and neither party had an interest in representing their distinct interests.

PRESIDENT HERBERT HOOVER AND THE BLACK FRUSTRATION WITH THE TWO-PARTY SYSTEM

In 1928, African-Americans faced the prospect of a presidential election in which both contenders were hostile toward them.

Once again the Republican presidential candidate vied for the allegiance of southern whites. And Democratic presidential nominee, Governor Alfred E. Smith of New York, had the reputation as a liberal, but he personally remained mute with respect to blacks.[49]

The campaign began in Houston, Texas, where the 1928 Democratic National Convention was held. The tone of the convention was set by a lynching that occurred outside. And inside the convention, African-American alternates and attendees found themselves encaged within wire fencing in order to segregate them from the white Democrats. There were no full-fledged black delegates, with black participation being limited to a 100-person choir.[50]

Walter White, head of the NAACP, initially supported Alfred Smith in his campaign against Herbert Hoover, but he grew disappointed with the Democratic Party.

Meanwhile, black frustration with the Republican Party and their presidential candidate, Herbert Hoover, was at an all-time high. At one point, the Smith campaign launched an effort to win black support and enlisted Walter White of the National Association for the Advancement of Colored People (NAACP) to lead the effort. White said that Smith was "the best man for the Presidency" and that "his enemies . . . are the Negroes' enemies."[51] The enthusiastic White believed that the Republican stranglehold on African-American national electoral politics would be loosened if not broken.

Later, White grew disillusioned with Smith and the Democrats whose virulent anti-black practices led to the nomination of a southerner as their vice-presidential candidate. White's dismay was expressed in a letter to a friend that specifically mentioned the "putting of Negro spectators at Houston in a caged enclosure."[52] Nevertheless, he was motivated by a naive belief that the "NAACP will be the power behind the throne" and that black political independence would boost black power.[53] Eventually, White abandoned this course, as the Democratic campaign's determined anti-black edge made it impossible.[54] African-Americans asked Smith to make a strong statement in support of the principles of democracy, for protection of the right to vote, against the practice of lynching, and for equal educational opportunity. Smith not only refused, he didn't utter a single word that could be construed as friendly to African-Americans.

Smith received substantial black voter support in some cities such as Philadelphia where he received 17 percent in the predominantly black wards. In Harlem, the share garnered by the Democratic presidential candidate had increased from 3 percent in 1920 to 28 percent in 1924 and 1928.[55] This contest, however, was one in which both candidates held black interests in contempt. W. E. B. DuBois summed up the sentiments of many black citizens when he said, "it does not matter a tinker's damn which of these gentlemen succeed."[56]

Renowned editor and writer W. E. B. DuBois recognized that neither the Republicans nor the Democrats were truly friends to African-Americans.

Both candidates did their utmost to appeal to the anti-black sentiments of white voters. The restructuring of southern Republican Party organizations was an important component of Hoover's campaign strategy in this respect. Hoover's purge of African-Americans from southern branches of his party would complete their banishment from the politics of the region. At the 1928 Republican National Convention, the Hoover-controlled credentials committee refused to seat Florida black delegates, replacing them with the "lily-white" white candidates from that state. This scenario was repeated in state after state as black delegates from the south were replaced by white delegates. The black-and-tan delegates were replaced by members of the rival lily-white southern delegations.[57]

After Mississippi's Governor Theodore G. Bilbo spread the rumor than Hoover had danced with Mary Booze, an African-American national Republican committeewoman from Mound Bayou, Mississippi, the ensuing Republican reaction was revealing. An aide to Hoover called this the "most indecent and unworthy statement in the whole of a bitter campaign."[58] Taking advantage of his position as head of the Commerce Department, Hoover shrewdly desegregated the department just prior to the 1928 presidential election.[59] Hoover's maneuver and overall strategy paid off as he won seven southern states and still managed to gather a majority of black northern votes.[60]

Herbert Clark Hoover was born in August 1874 in West Branch, Iowa, to Quaker parents. He was raised in a racially liberal atmosphere for the period. However, that liberalism seemed largely forgotten when, as a young engineer in China, he wrote that the "simply appalling and universal dishonesty of the [Chinese] working classes, the racial slowness, and the low average of intelligence, gives them an efficiency far below the workmen of England and America. . . ."[61] In his book *Principles of Mining*, Hoover indicated his belief that blacks were less intelligent and ambitious than whites. Furthermore, he made clear his opposition to interracial marriages of whites to blacks or Asians.[62]

In his 1930 nomination of Judge John J. Parker of North Carolina to the U.S. Supreme Court, Hoover ran into opposition from African-Americans.[63] In an effort to shore up his white southern support, Hoover nominated a man who believed that African-Americans should be permanently excluded from American political life. Parker contended that the level of black culture, character, and intelligence was beneath that required for political participation. He called black political involvement "a source of evil and [a] danger to both races and is not desired by the wise men of either race or by the Republican Party of North Carolina."[64] Ultimately, President Hoover's nomination of Judge Parker to the U.S. Supreme Court was defeated. Hoover's two subsequent nominations to the Supreme Court did nothing to narrow the gulf between his administration and African-Americans.[65]

Another incident incensed the national black community against the Hoover administration. A group of mothers of soldiers killed in World War I were sent on a trip to Europe, where they were to attend a ceremony. This event was marred by the revelations of a humiliating segregation of black mothers from white mothers. The white mothers would sail on well-equipped U.S. Navy ships, while black mothers would sail on rougher "cattle boats." President Hoover had the option of intervening, to ensure that blacks would have, at least, "separate but equal" facilities, but he chose not to.[66]

Hoover did not attack segregation in the nation's capital, in the armed forces, or in the South in general.[67] While Hoover took more positive actions in favor of blacks and black interests than Harding and Coolidge had, many of these attempts were token, and they were offset by a number of negative and damaging actions.

PRESIDENT FRANKLIN D. ROOSEVELT AND THE NEW DEAL FOR AFRICAN-AMERICANS

Facing the specter of 100,000 militant African-Americans marching in the segregated nation's capital, President Franklin Delano Roosevelt gave in to the demands for a federal Fair Employment Practices Committee (FEPC) and additional jobs in the booming wartime industries.[68] Only ten years before, this would have been an unimaginable scenario and outcome: African-Americans pressuring a Democratic president, whom they overwhelmingly supported, to desegregate the massive employment structures of the defense industries and the armed forces.

Escalating their preparations for war in the late 1930s, many of Europe's great powers purchased weapons from the United States, serving to jump-start American industry. African-Americans, "the last hired and first fired" during the Depression, were especially eager to share in the benefits of the newly thriving economy. Yet, they were almost completely excluded from the defense industry and remained segregated within an expanding military. When blacks were hired in the defense industries, they were confined to the designated "Negro" jobs. And while in the armed forces, they were restricted to segregated camps and lowly ranks.[69] When the gloom of the Depression lifted for white Americans, for black Americans it persisted. Black opinion was becoming more agitated and militant in relation to this issue. Communication between the White House and black leadership had broken down, leading the NAACP to plan a massive march on Washington for July 1941. The protest would address the issues of segregation in the armed forces and exclusion from the defense industries.[70]

Born in January 1882, Franklin Delano Roosevelt spent much of his childhood in the company of his parents, and he was supervised closely. Roosevelt's ancestry went deep into the early settlement of the nation, and by the era of the American Revolution the family was already wealthy.

The nomination of Roosevelt was initially a disappointment to African-Americans, who were desperately searching for an alternative to the Republican Party. FDR's 1932 strategy entailed cultivating ties to southern Democratic state parties and avoiding being associated with northern black Democrats. Roosevelt's choice for his vice-presidential running mate, Texan John Nance Garner—hailing from Uvalde, Texas, where it was forbidden for blacks to live—alienated the future president from the black electorate.[71]

Nevertheless, African-Americans gave an unprecedented level of support to Democratic presidential candidate Roosevelt.[72] While an estimated 30 percent of African-Americans supported Roosevelt in 1932, by 1936 some 75 percent of blacks would cast their votes for him as an incumbent.[73]

The Depression-era programs were rife with various forms of racism. The National Recovery Administration (NRA) was established by the National Industrial Recovery Act as a key link in the strategy for national economic recovery. From the inception of the agency, blacks hoped that its employment practices would be free from racial bias. Roosevelt administration officials encouraged this optimism by assuring that race would not be a factor in hiring and promotion. Racism proved too entrenched, however, and Roosevelt's will too weak, to overturn decades-old racially exploitative patterns. The new labor code failed to cover a large portion of the jobs in which African-Americans were most heavily represented.

Through a complex web of eligibility for coverage, the NRA minimum wage scales bypassed blacks. In cotton mills, for

Many years after slavery, some African-Americans remained in the cotton fields but as tenant farmers.

example, "cleaners" and "outside employees"—occupational categories that the vast majority of blacks fell into—were excluded from NRA coverage.[74] The NRA's significance for African-Americans was that prices rose without a corresponding rise in income. In addition, the codes failed to cover the thousands of black workers who worked as domestics; continued to pay the depressed wages typically paid to blacks in the South; and had no safeguards against the racially motivated firings that resulted from the raising of the wages paid to black workers.[75] T. Arnold Hill, a National Urban League aide, felt that "the will of those who have kept Negroes in economic disfranchisement has been permitted to prevail, and the government has looked on in silence and at times with approval. Consequently, the Negro worker has good reason to feel that this government has betrayed him under the New Deal."[76]

The Depression hit blacks in southern rural areas particularly hard. More than one analyst has concluded that the Agricultural Adjustment Administration (AAA) and NRA "failed conspicuously to relieve the distress" of African-American workers and farmers.[77] Southern white landowners feared that the program would increase the independence of black tenant farmers. The Roosevelt administration took their prejudices and desires for continued domination into full consideration. The federal program managers acquiesced to the racist traditions of the region and suggested cotton contracts giving landowners four and a half cents for every pound (.4 kilogram) of cotton not grown and tenants one-half cent for every pound (.4 kg) of cotton not grown. In other parts of the nation for other crops, such divisions were on the order of fifty-fifty.[78] The impact of the AAA crop reduction program was disastrous and led to the displacement of African-American sharecroppers and tenants.[79] By 1940, there were 192,000 less African-American tenant farmers than in 1930, partially as a result of the AAA program.[80]

The NAACP and other black activist organizations recommended that the crop reduction payments be given directly to the tenants, and they suggested the appointment of blacks to help administer the program. The majority of these recommendations were rejected by the Roosevelt administration.[81] The Civilian Conservation Corps (CCC) was also organized along lines amenable to the white southern elite. Initially, the benefits flowed almost exclusively to whites, as blacks were excluded from the vast majority of camps. Only 3 percent of the first 250,000 CCC recruits were black.[82] Pressure from the NAACP and other groups succeeded in forcing the recruitment of an increased number of blacks. Nevertheless, a very low glass ceiling led to few blacks at the agency in positions of authority.[83]

Following the refusal of the Daughters of the American Revolution (DAR) to rent Constitutional Hall to the famed African-American contralto Marian Anderson, Roosevelt's Department of Interior made the Lincoln Memorial available for a large open-air concert. Later, Eleanor Roosevelt presented Anderson with the NAACP's Spingarn Medal. These events helped to cement the ties binding African-Americans to the Roosevelt administration and his Democratic Party.[84]

Walter White of the NAACP met with Roosevelt to push for his support of anti-lynching legislation. White's discussion with the president was preceded by a more favorable encounter with his wife, Eleanor. FDR tried to avoid discussing the issue, and when forced to respond to White's arguments, admitted that he was unwilling to confront the power of the southern wing of the Democratic party about this issue.[85]

Eleanor Roosevelt presenting contralto Marian Anderson with the NAACP's Spingarn Medal in 1939

White tried to convince Roosevelt to use the expanded Lindberg law to indict participants in lynchings. Motivating White was the 1934 murder of Claude Neal, who was kidnapped from a jail in Brewton, Alabama, and taken to Florida where he was lynched. Advertised in local newspapers and radio programs, the lynching was attended by thousands of spectators. No federal investigation or prosecution followed.[86] Later, however, when the growing black political power and electoral clout had became more evident, the Roosevelt administration would occasionally order the FBI to investigate civil rights violations. In 1942, the Justice Department investigated a lynching for the first time: the brutal Missouri lynching of Cleo Wright.[87]

Yet at a press conference only days after the 1934 Neal lynching, President Roosevelt was asked whether he supported the anti-lynching bill then pending before Congress. Roosevelt avoided answering the question by pleading for time to review his policy, claiming to have forgotten his past actions. Roy Wilkins attacked what he viewed as Roosevelt's "expedient cowardice."

Powerful southern opposition to the measure launched a filibuster in January 1938. Lynching was defended by southern senators as a necessary measure "to protect the fair womanhood of the South from beasts."[88] It took the horrible lynching of two African-Americans with a blowtorch to shock the U.S. Congress into finally passing anti-lynching legislation in early 1938. Roosevelt, who in a 1933 address condemned lynching as "collective murder," now heeded the increased urban political power of the black community and supported passage of the legislation. Then in February, Roosevelt caved in to the wishes of the southern senators, citing the need to pass emergency relief legislation. Once again, the political expediency of pursuing issues deemed to be of higher priority took precedent over a vital issue of black survival. Yet, anti-lynching legislation and enforcement was closer, and some observers regarded this as tangible progress.[89]

On April 12, 1945, Franklin Delano Roosevelt died, leaving Harry S. Truman to take the helm.[90] Energized by their experiences in war, depression, and racial strife, African-Americans faced the challenges of the postwar period with greater confidence in the future than ever before. More than ever this confidence stemmed from the sense of their own power, rather than the politics and personality of the person who sat in the Oval Office.

CHAPTER FIVE

AMERICAN PRESIDENTS DURING THE CIVIL RIGHTS ERA

HARRY TRUMAN: THE IMPERATIVES OF THE COLD WAR AND RACE

Speaking in 1940 before an all-white audience in Sedalia, Missouri, Harry S. Truman, who was running for reelection to the Senate, openly proclaimed:

> *I believe in the brotherhood of man, not merely the brotherhood of white men but the brotherhood of all men before law.*

The Missouri senator recounted the past decades of "lynching and mob violence, lack of schools, and countless other unfair conditions" stimulating a migration into the cities.

> *The majority of our Negro people find cold comfort in shanties and tenements. Surely, as freemen, they are entitled to something better than this.*[1]

Truman's memorable speech at Sedalia was not an aberration; it represented the evolving politics of a senator sensitive to black voting opinion. The 130,000-plus African-American voting population of Kansas City and St. Louis stood poised to make Truman pay for any backsliding on equal rights.

Born to John Anderson and Martha Ellen Young Truman in 1884, the future president was raised in Grandview, and Independence, Missouri. Harry Truman was steeped in an atmosphere of racial prejudice. In a letter to his future wife Bess in 1911, Truman unabashedly wrote:

I think one man is just as good as another so long as he's honest and decent and not a nigger or a Chinaman. Uncle Will says that the Lord made a white man from dust, a nigger from mud, then He threw up what was left and it came down a Chinaman.[2]

Truman continued to write that his uncle hated "Chinese and Japs" commenting, "So do I." While admitting this was "race prejudice," he nevertheless believed that "Negroes ought to be in Africa, yellow men in Asia and white men in Europe and America."[3]

Some four decades later, President Truman received the 1949 Negro Newspaper Publishers Association's John B. Russwurm Award for "his courageous leadership and uncompromising stand in the fight for civil rights."[4] As never before, the U.S. government and political establishment were sensitive to the images of U.S. society that were broadcast abroad. In a majority "colored" world, the image of a United States, with a long history of slavery and hostile to non-white peoples, threatened to tilt the balance of international power toward the Soviet Union.[5]

In September 1946, Truman met with an organization that requested that he issue a strong statement against lynching. Subsequently, President Truman, speaking to an annual Urban League meeting, declared that America "must not . . . and shall not remain indifferent in the face of acts of intimidation and violence in our . . . communities."[6]

Truman warily endorsed a permanent FEPC. The new agency, however, was crippled from birth by the lack of funding, staff, and authority.[7] During the FEPC's five years of existence, some 14,000 discrimination complaints were filed by African-Americans and only nine of the 35 enforcement orders issued by the FEPC were respected by employers.[8] Occasionally, Truman personally obstructed efforts to end job discrimination. In the fall of 1945—after the Truman administration countermanded a government move to seize the Capital Transit Company in order to force an end to its policy of racial discrimination—one member of the FEPC resigned in anger over this action. Stressing Truman's legal obligation to enforce the policies of non-discrimination in employment, he charged the president with condoning racism.[9]

The political problem for President Truman, however, was that he was faced with the task of holding together a shaky Democratic coalition based on labor, African-Americans, and white southerners. In this respect, President Truman displayed a determination not to alienate his southern Democratic constituency. For example, Truman's Justice Department watched as the forces of Herman Talmadge, a candidate for governor of Georgia, engaged in the wholesale removal of blacks from the state's voting rolls. Despite the FBI's knowledge of this, no arrests or prosecutions were attempted.[10] At the same time that no action was taken in instances of gross violations of black civil rights, the FBI expended considerable resources in the surveillance of the NAACP's activities.[11] In 1949, Paul Robeson criticized the appointment of Attorney General Tom Clark to the Supreme Court as a "gratuitous and outrageous insult to my people." Robeson pointed out that Clark, in his capacity as attorney general, had placed several civil rights organizations on the list of subversives.[12]

At the 1948 Democratic National Convention, Truman tried to ease the concerns of southern segregationists but was pressured by the urban, black, and liberal forces for a stronger anti-discrimination platform position.[13] The presidential campaign of 1948 marked a new awareness among politicians of the importance of the black vote. The campaign featured an unprecedented competition for the African-American vote. Republican Thomas E. Dewey, Progressive Party presidential candidate Henry Wallace, and Truman vied for black votes.[14] While Truman had relied on black votes for practically his entire political career, he realized in 1948 that he especially needed to appeal to this constituency in order to win the presidency. The dreaded prospect of African-Americans deciding a presidential election appeared the first time in U.S. history. This reality served to spur Truman to initiate a flurry of racially progressive measures, including the issuing of Executive Order 9981 in July 1948, which established a policy of "equality of treatment and opportunity" within the United States armed forces.[15] The latter action largely resulted from the pressure exerted by another March on Washington movement launched by A. Phillip Randolph.[16] Yet, it also proved key to his eventual victory at the polls. Truman's narrow victories in California, Illinois, and Ohio were critical and were made possible by his plurality among the states' black voters.[17]

PRESIDENT EISENHOWER AND THE CIVIL RIGHTS MOVEMENT

Discharged after three years of service in the South Pacific, Isaac Woodward was on a bus headed home to North Carolina from a camp in Georgia when he requested to use the restroom

Segregation existed throughout the South, even on public buses.

during a stop. When he reboarded the bus, Woodward was verbally abused for taking too long. Then, at another rest stop in South Carolina, the bus driver asked police to arrest Woodward, claiming he was drunk and disorderly. Protesting that this was not the case, Woodward was so brutally assaulted that he was blinded for life. Later, the police chief responsible for the beating was acquitted.[18]

The case of Isaac Woodward exemplifies the dangers interstate travel held for African-Americans during the postwar period. Not only were African-Americans routinely terrorized by random acts of racial violence during the immediate aftermath of World War II, they remained under the yoke of Jim Crow in every other public sphere of life. During the previous two decades, some progress had been made in advancing African-American political, social, and economic status. Yet, the hard core of the institutional framework of the Jim Crow order remained intact with its besieged defenders battling with renewed determination. By any measure, the black condition remained that of an oppressed, semi-free people chained by tenancy, debt peonage, unequal education, political disfranchisement, and social degradation. Public space in American life—including museums, schools, parks, restaurants, public transportation, and other vital institutions—remained riddled with segregation.

Increasingly, incidents involving African diplomats would expose the pervasiveness and immorality of racism in American society. In October 1957, H. A. Gbedemah, the finance minister of newly independent Ghana was ejected from a Howard Johnson's restaurant in Dover, Delaware. Insulted, Gbedemah was told that black people were not served. This soon mushroomed into an international incident that further damaged the worldwide image of U.S. society.[19] President Dwight Eisenhower was reportedly angered by the incident and immediately invited the Ghanian official to have breakfast with him at the White House.[20]

PRESIDENT EISENHOWER: SYMPATHY FOR THE SOUTH

Campaigning in October 1952 against Democrat Adlai Stevenson, General Dwight Eisenhower focused upon winning the allegiance of southern and border-state whites. The Republican presidential candidate's strength was bolstered by the solid support from South Carolina Governor James F. Byrnes, and Senator Harry F. Byrd of Virginia. Using "Dixie" as a southern theme song, Eisenhower reminded southerners that he had opposed the FEPC and stood against integration.

President Eisenhower, meeting here with both black and white leaders, seemed to waver in his opinion of integration.

To northern audiences perceived as more liberal on race, Eisenhower presented a more moderate image, playing down his basic opposition to integration. In Wheeling, Virginia, Eisenhower advocated the end of segregation in the military and the District of Columbia, and he spoke in favor of black enfranchisement. In October 1952, Eisenhower declared that he stood for "true equality of opportunity for all men," expressing impatience for the "idea of second-class citizenship."[21]

Despite Eisenhower's occasional flurries of racially liberal rhetoric, his overall tilt to the white South was readily discerned by the African-American press. C. A. Franklin, writing in the *Call* newspaper, termed Eisenhower a "changeling" who vainly tried to woo both northern blacks and southern racists.[22] On the eve of the election, an unknown group dropped anti-African-American leaflets from planes into southern cities. Following this incident, the NAACP pressed Eisenhower to condemn this tactic, but to no avail.[23]

During Eisenhower's distinguished military career, he once encountered a black Illinois National Guardsman whom he perceived "just couldn't do anything."[24] This particular soldier made him doubt how capable or motivated blacks could be. The general later testified before a congressional committee in 1948 that he stood against desegregation, citing its unworkable nature. The future president expressed his belief that "if we attempt merely by passing a lot of laws to force someone to like someone else, we are just going to get into trouble."[25] In a larger sense, Eisenhower didn't believe in social integration between blacks and whites, disagreeing with the notion that "a Negro should court my daughter."[26]

President Eisenhower was disheartened by the upsurge in protest activity by African-Americans during his administration. Spurred on by the May 17, 1954, Supreme Court *Brown v. Board of Education* decision that outlawed segregated schools, black activism began to succeed. South Carolina Governor Jimmy Byrnes told the president that whites in his state were "frightened at putting the children together."[27] While President Eisenhower initially took an official stance of neutrality on *Brown*, he later told Chief Justice Earl Warren that southerners "are not bad people." "All they are concerned about is to see that their sweet little girls are not required to sit in school alongside some big overgrown Negroes."[28]

President Eisenhower, thoroughly frustrated by the persistence of the issue of black civil rights, saw his worst fears materialized in the 1957 Little Rock, Arkansas, crisis. The president lamented, "You cannot change the hearts of people by law." The key problem to Eisenhower was that the impact of the decision was "cutting into established customs and traditions of such communities as Little Rock."[29]

President Eisenhower reluctantly federalized the Arkansas National Guard and sent federal troops to Little Rock, Arkansas, after both the National Guard and white mobs prevented the enrollment of nine black students. Despite this action, Eisenhower was convinced that blacks sought progress too fast. Once he told an anecdote concerning the state of black unrest in the south. In it a southern black said, "If someone doesn't shut up around here, particularly these Negroes from the North, they're going to get a lot of us niggers killed!"[30]

The most important African-American in Eisenhower's administration was E. Frederic Morrow, who delivered more than 300 speeches in service to the administration. Morrow recounted a "tongue lashing" given to him by Max Rabb during the 1956 campaign. Reflecting a common sentiment within the Eisenhower administration, Rabb told Morrow that blacks were ungrateful to the president. Rabb advised Morrow to "walk softly from then on and ask fewer questions of the members of the Administration on this matter."[31]

Morrow wrote that any suggestion for Eisenhower to speak out against the unruly white mobs was greeted with "complete fright" and noted his silence on the lynching of Emmett Till in Mississippi in 1955.[32] In 1956, the president concluded that it would be inadvisable to meet with A. Phillip Randolph because it "would incense southern governors" among others.[33] In May 1958, President Eisenhower spoke before the African-American National Newspaper Publishers' Association and declared: "No one is more anxious than I am to see Negroes receive first-class citizenship in this country . . . but you must be patient."[34]

JOHN F. KENNEDY: CAPTURING THE BLACK VOTE

Arrested on October 19, 1960, with 52 other African-Americans in an effort to desegregate Atlanta's Rich department store,

Martin Luther King, Jr. was immediately rearrested upon his release. Charged with violating parole stemming from an earlier traffic violation, King was sentenced to four months of hard labor, plunging the nation into a sense of impending crisis as concern for King's safety reverberated across the nation and the world. Occurring during the heat of a tight presidential race between Vice President Richard M. Nixon and Massachusetts Senator John Fitzgerald Kennedy, King's arrest had an immediate impact on the campaign. Both camps faced the question of how to respond to King's arrest, and both candidates feared the loss of southern support by appearing to support African-American de-

Martin Luther King, Jr., and his followers strove to influence the presidency.

mands for desegregation and equality. Vice President Nixon was especially torn by this decision, and in the end, Nixon failed to issue a statement in support of King's release.[35]

John F. Kennedy, in contrast, reached an agreement with Georgia's Governor, Ernest Vandiver. Vandiver committed himself to obtaining the release of King in exchange for a promise that no statement would be issued. Kennedy later telephoned Coretta Scott King to express his sympathy.[36] Kennedy's symbolic gesture solidified his support among blacks. Martin Luther King, Sr., the African-American leader's father, switched his allegiance to Kennedy and commented, "Because this man was willing to wipe the tears from my daughter-in-law's eyes, I've got a suitcase of votes, and I'm going to take them to Mr. Kennedy and dump them in his lap."[37] The Kennedy campaign moved quickly to take advantage of the political bonanza: one million pamphlets celebrating Kennedy's phone call were distributed around the nation in African-American communities. One half million were given out in Chicago alone. On the Sunday prior to the election, these pamphlets were distributed outside African-American churches throughout the nation.[38]

The importance of Kennedy's timely symbolic gesture was illustrated by the narrowness of his victory. In Illinois, Kennedy, winning by only 9,000 votes, found the 250,000 black votes from the state indispensable. Similarly, Kennedy's victory in South Carolina, by only 10,000 votes, was made possible by an estimated 40,000 black votes.[39] Overall, African-Americans gave Kennedy 70 percent of their votes, enabling him to achieve a narrow victory over the Republican Nixon.[40]

John F. Kennedy was born on May 29, 1917, in Brookline, Massachusetts. As an emerging national figure, the young Kennedy was not especially liberal. He once said, "I'd be very happy to tell them I'm not a liberal at all."[41] Kennedy faced his first major political test of his commitment to racial equality in 1957 when the Senate debated a civil rights bill. He allied himself with the southern Democrats who sent the bill to the Senate Judiciary Committee, whose chairman, Senator James Eastland (D-Miss), was a fierce opponent of black equality. As late as 1956, he adhered to a view of Reconstruction that harshly condemned the northern role. In Kennedy's *Profiles in Courage*, Radical Republican Thaddeus Stevens is described as "the crippled, fanatical personification of the extremes of the Radical Republic movement."[42]

Offering a tantalizing vision of his presidency before the eyes of candidate-starved blacks, Kennedy on July 10, 1960, addressed a NAACP rally in Los Angeles. The presidential candidate identified himself with "courage and candor" on the civil rights issue, brooking "no compromise of basic principles—no evasion of basic controversies—and no second-class citizenship for any American."[43]

Senator Kennedy's speech entitled "The Standard of John C. Calhoun" only months later calls into question the sincerity of the candidate's promises of candor, forthrightness, and principle on issues of black civil rights. Kennedy began this Columbia, South Carolina, campaign speech by an extended comparison of two "great" American senators: Daniel Webster of Massachusetts and John C. Calhoun of South Carolina. The latter figure distinguished himself by his commitment to maintaining Africans in perpetual slavery. Kennedy, playing the race card, deftly used Calhoun as a not-so-subtle symbol of racism in order to win white southern support.[44]

When Martin Luther King and John F. Kennedy met in June 1960, King was impressed after learning that two prominent white liberal friends were on Kennedy's campaign staff. King maintained a determined neutrality, pointing out the major faults of both candidates and the history of broken promises to black Americans by politicians. The African-American leader commented that "both major parties have been hypocritical on the question of civil rights" and have used his people as "a political football."[45] Later, King made President Kennedy his personal "project," as he was determined over time to reform the president's views toward greater racial liberalism.[46]

THE KENNEDY ADMINISTRATION AND CIVIL RIGHTS

Amid the lofty phrases and rhetoric of President John F. Kennedy's inaugural address, none concerned the hopes and aspirations of African-Americans. Within the first two weeks of the new administration, Martin Luther King outlined in *The Nation* a comprehensive agenda of African-American interests for the new president. King recommended three activities for the Kennedy administration to foster black civil rights: "resolute presidential leadership" legislatively; "moral persuasion"; and the use of executive orders.[47] King pointed out that executive orders could also immediately end racial bias in employment in federal agencies and departments.

Despite this plea by King, Kennedy relegated the issues surrounding black civil rights to a low priority. Several other domestic and international issues held his attention instead.[48] Early in his administration, Kennedy believed that he could go slow on civil rights and avoid pitting his two key constituencies against one another. Without the intervention of black activists, this course may have prevailed. However, the determination to integrate public accommodations foiled Kennedy's dreams of social peace. The violence that greeted their travels through the South forced Kennedy to act on behalf of black interests.[49]

Far from encouraging the assertiveness of the civil rights movement, the Kennedy administration acted to contain it, to pacify and tame it, so as not to destroy its political bonds with the white south. During the 1961 Freedom Rides crisis, Attorney General Robert F. Kennedy had a telephone conversation with Martin Luther King that highlighted the differences in perspectives, objectives, and philosophies between the two men. In a conversation that at times grew tense, King told the attorney general that the decision to refuse bail was "a matter of conscience and morality" in order to correct a social injustice. After King went so far as to suggest that it might be necessary to fill the jails to achieve the movement's objectives, Attorney General Kennedy took offense and told him bluntly not to threaten the administration. King commented later, "they don't understand the social revolution going on in the world, and therefore they don't understand what we're doing."[50]

The fear that the problems of black civil rights would pose an obstacle to U.S. foreign policy was fully realized during the Freedom Rides—protests that were made against segregation on public buses. At the very moment President Kennedy was meeting with Soviet Premier Nikita Khrushchev in Vienna, news of the Freedom Rides and their violent reception hit the international media. Immediately following a white mob's besieging of a Montgomery, Alabama, church that included Martin Luther King and a thousand others inside, Attorney General Robert F. Kennedy sought to have the Freedom Rides called off. He told black leaders that the nonviolent protest was embarrassing his brother in Vienna. Robert Kennedy's plea was to no avail, however, and soon he himself mandated the Interstate Commerce Commission to issue regulations desegregating interstate bus transportation.[51]

This refusal to commit himself more to the cause of the African-American movement for social, economic, and political justice was an important factor in Kennedy's relatively high standing in the polls in the white South. The Kennedy administration shared with the vast majority of its predecessors in the White House a "states' rights" position, contending that it was beyond the scope of the constitutional powers of the federal government to extend protection to African-American civil rights workers in the south. But certain events repeatedly forced the administration's hand.[52] Following the crisis surrounding James Meredith's enrollment in the University of Mississippi, the president's views underwent rapid change. Kennedy's old pro-southern sympathies began to be shed as he witnessed the irrationality of the white resistance to desegregation.[53]

The Kennedy administration sought to balance the desires of white southern and African-American supporters by diverting the civil rights movement into areas less threatening to white southerners.[54] Kennedy mistakenly believed that black disenfranchisement was less dear to the hearts of southern whites than were segregated drinking fountains, rest rooms, schools, and lunch counters. In order to effect the desired objectives,

President Kennedy (fourth from right) and members of his administration meeting with black leaders, including Martin Luther King, Jr. (fifth from left), A. Phillip Randolph (fifth from right), and Roy Wilkins (far right)

Kennedy offered foundation financial support.[55] At a June 1961 meeting that included activists and civil rights organizations, Attorney General Robert F. Kennedy promised not only foundation support, but also Justice Department support in fostering black voter registration campaigns in the south.[56]

The voter registration campaigns that escalated in the early 1960s were hardly the peaceful nondisruptive affairs President Kennedy had hoped for. Rather they touched the core of political power in the South, setting off explosions of conflict initiated by die-hard racists determined to maintain control. The Kennedy administration failed to honor its stated commitment to utilizing the Justice Department in protecting civil rights workers who were seeking to register black voters.[57]

The young activists of the Student Non-Violent Coordinating Committee (SNCC) found themselves taking up a decades-old endeavor to obtain federal government intervention in the South in order to secure African-American political rights. What angered SNCC activists was that blacks were legally entitled to vote and the Kennedy administration failed to live up to its promises of support, even when the very lives of the activists were threatened.[58]

PRESIDENT KENNEDY AND THE MARCH ON WASHINGTON

An early 1963 *Nation* article by Martin Luther King accused the Kennedy administration of holding back civil rights progress. King complained that the "demand for progress was somehow drained of its moral imperative, and the issue no longer commanded the conscience of the nation as it had in previous years."[59] Later, the increasing tensions between the Kennedy administration and the African-American community exploded in a confrontation between black activists and Attorney General Robert F. Kennedy at author James Baldwin's New York apartment.[60]

Deeply moved by the protests and violence in Birmingham, President Kennedy addressed the nation on June 11, 1963, and announced the submission of a new civil rights bill to Congress. Kennedy contended that the United States was founded "on the principle that all men are created equal, and that the rights of every man are diminished when the rights of one man are threatened."[61] Perhaps heeding the counsel of Martin Luther King, Kennedy described the cause of racial justice in moral terms declaring, "We are confronted primarily with a moral issue," one "as old as the Scriptures" and "as clear as the American Constitution."[62] Clearly, Kennedy's effort to influence the civil rights movement failed; King's and the civil rights movement's efforts to change Kennedy did not.[63]

In 1963, a wave of black activism—taking the newly popular forms of sit-ins, demonstrations, marches, and boycotts— swept the South, and, increasingly, the North. One estimate, by the Southern Regional Council, was that 930 "public protest demonstrations" occurred in 115 cities in 11 states during 1963.[64] African-Americans were on the move, seemingly an unstoppable force as every week new battles were engaged by militant activists. African-Americans were themselves transformed by their new thrust for basic civil rights and the white resistance to their demands. Racial polarization became more evident as whites increasingly concluded that blacks wanted progress "too fast" at the same time that blacks were increasingly impatient with the status quo.

Eventually, Kennedy's reluctant civil rights measures cut into his southern support, as reflected in the polls. In September 1963, the Gallup Poll indicated his approval rating in the South plummeted from 60 percent in March of 1963 to 44 percent in September as some 70 percent of southern whites felt that his pursuit of integration was too hurried.[65]

At the same time, the prestige of black nationalist politics grew steadily in the north. The prospect of a massive black march on Washington tied to related actions, according to Malcolm X, "scared the white man to death."[66] Kennedy's effort to co-opt

Malcolm X was a strong voice for African-Americans during the civil rights movement.

the march by linking it to white liberals and foundations transformed it into "a picnic, a circus," replete with "clowns and all."[67]

Failing to have the march canceled, Kennedy endorsed it and attempted to constrain it. As the Kennedy administration and the NAACP's Roy Wilkins intervened in the preparations, the tone of the March changed dramatically. Disruption and radicalism were out, and moderation was in. Foundations became major financial backers of the events, and the Kennedy administration became a part of the planning. Bayard Rustin was replaced by A. Phillip Randolph as the head of the march, as the former was deemed by Wilkins to be too radical. Supporting Malcolm X's contention that the march represented a "farce on Washington" and on African-Americans, the Kennedy administration was prepared to disconnect the public address system if the wrong phrases were uttered.[68]

Following the march, President Kennedy congratulated march organizers on the peacefulness of the event (he had thousands of troops standing by if plans went awry), and he met with some at the White House. He greeted the march's leaders at the White House, welcoming King with the phrase, "I have a dream."[69] King's own celebration was monitored by the wiretap approved by the president at J. Edgar Hoover's behest.[70]

On November 22, 1963, the Kennedy Administration came to a sudden end. At age 47, John F. Kennedy was slain in Dallas by an assassin's bullet.

Martin Luther King, Jr., delivering his "I Have a Dream" speech during the 1963 March on Washington

LYNDON B. JOHNSON: THE TRANSFORMATION OF A SEGREGATIONIST

Speaking to a rally in Austin in 1947, ambitious young Senator Lyndon B. Johnson harshly attacked proposed civil rights measures, calling President Truman's civil rights program "a farce and a sham." Not coincidentally, he opposed the anti-lynching bill since the "federal government has no more business enacting a law against one kind of murder than another." He also opposed the FEPC, contending that it violated the rights of employers.[71]

Less than two decades later, however, President Lyndon Baines Johnson presided over the most important series of legislative measures in the history of the United States. Most remarkably, these were key measures to enhance the status of African-Americans. For the fifth consecutive presidential administration, the sheer power of the African-American freedom movement compelled the chief executive to implement a minimum of reform to restore social stability.

Lyndon Baines Johnson was born in 1908 near Austin in Texas Hill Country. As a young congressman, Johnson voted with his fellow southerners and opposed measures to end the scourge of lynching, to abolish poll taxes, and to end employment discrimination in the federal government. During this period, Johnson fell back on "states' rights" as a justification for these political positions.[72] As Johnson grew increasingly concerned with a national constituency, he recognized that a die-hard commitment to Jim Crow was politically limiting and he slowly began distancing himself from his southern colleagues.[73]

On August 4, 1964 three civil rights workers were found murdered in Philadelphia, Mississippi. Their disappearance and the subsequent publicity forced the federal government to send 200 naval personnel and 150 FBI agents to join the search. President Johnson, while directing the massive search, nevertheless carefully avoided involvement in "local" southern affairs.[74]

Despite the lack of federal intervention to protect black voters and voting rights activists in the South during 1964, the militants of the SNCC pinned their hopes on unseating the lily-white Mississippi Democratic delegation at the party's national convention in Atlantic City. In April 1964, these youthful civil rights workers helped found the Mississippi Freedom Democratic Party (MFDP) in Jackson, Mississippi, in order to displace the segregated state Democratic Party.[75] The activists reasoned that their principles were more in accord with the national party, who had opposed much of Johnson's domestic policies, and that the all-white composition of the traditional delegation was an affront to the civil rights principles of the party.[76] President Johnson, however, feared the loss of southern support and assured Governor Paul B. Johnson of Mississippi of his opposition to the MFDP. He put the MFDP activists under FBI surveillance and refused to discuss his support for the segregationist delegation.[77]

President Johnson rejected a suggestion of a compromise made by MFDP adviser Joseph Rauh to seat both delegations. Fannie Lou Hamer, a SNCC and MFDP activist, delivered a moving speech to the convention recounting her brutal beating in jail. She challenged the convention declaring, "if the Freedom Democratic Party is not seated now, I question America."[78] The ensuing support forced Johnson to put forth a compromise proposal of allowing MFDP participation without voting rights. After this was rejected by the MFDP, the Johnson administration proposed that two MFDP delegates be accepted while the others were merely allowed to be present. Malcolm X concluded that at the heart of the problem was President Johnson. Terming him the "head of the Cracker Party," X said that Johnson "could have gotten Mrs. Hamer into Atlantic City," but he was "playing the same game" with his fellow white southerners.[79]

President Johnson went all out to ensure the passage of the 1964 Civil Rights Act. This was a key decision for the Texan, since it meant the probable loss of white support, especially in the south. The day after he signed the measure, Johnson told aide Bill Moyers, "I think we delivered the South to the Republican Party for your lifetime and mine."[80]

The longest filibuster in the history of the United States Congress occurred over the 1964 Civil Rights Act. The power flowing from the position and seniority of southern senators was formidable in the generally conservative body.[81] Yet, with arm-twisting and behind-the-scenes maneuvers, President Johnson smashed the southern filibuster. A signing ceremony that included major civil rights figures took place on July 2, 1964.

President Johnson's influence with black leaders was subsequently demonstrated following the outbreak of rioting in Harlem just two weeks after the signing of the 1964 Civil Rights Act. At Johnson's request, Martin Luther King, Roy Wilkins, and Whitney Young called for their "members voluntarily to observe a broad curtailment if not total moratorium of all mass marches, picketing and demonstrations until after Election Day, November 3."[82]

In the 1964 presidential election, President Johnson won reelection by a margin of almost 17 million votes, garnering 61 percent of the electorate vote, the highest percentage of popular vote in the history of presidential elections.[83] The black vote was key nevertheless; in several southern states newly enfranchised blacks voted for Johnson in overwhelming proportions, allowing him to win those states.[84]

THE PASSAGE OF THE VOTING RIGHTS ACT

On March 15, 1965, President Johnson made a major address to Congress entitled "The American Promise." In it, he clearly illustrated the fact that, in practical political terms, his racial liberalism surpassed that of his predecessor John F. Kennedy. Unlike Kennedy's, Johnson's liberalism was infused with the

President Johnson (seated) signing the Voting Rights Act in 1965

New Deal anti-poverty social welfare programs, making it of more day-to-day importance to African-Americans. In this speech, Johnson told Americans that their obligation to realize the objective of assuring every citizen's right to vote was based on the Constitution. Johnson assured the nation that this guarantee would benefit "not just Negroes" but the entire nation. He ended his address with a phrase of powerful symbolism: "And We Shall Overcome."[85]

Speaking in favor of the Voting Rights Act at Howard University on June 4, 1965, President Johnson stressed that his goal was "not just equality as a right and a theory but equality as a fact and equality as a result."[86] This speech represented a historical high-water mark of American presidential consciousness of black oppression; it acknowledged the impact slavery, its harsh aftermath, and contemporary racial injustice have had in restricting opportunities for African-Americans.[87]

On August 6, 1965, Johnson signed the Voting Rights Act in the Capitol Rotunda and was surrounded by well-known political and civil rights figures.[88] Less than one week later, the outbreak of serious rioting by African-Americans in the Los

Angeles section of Watts stunned President Johnson. August 11, 1965, was a day that deeply disillusioned Johnson. Only five days after the historic Voting Rights Act had been signed, the African-Americans in Watts indicated with profound deeds that this was too little and too late for their satisfaction.

Following the outbreak of the Watts riot, President Johnson remained in denial for a time. "How is it possible after all we've accomplished? How could it be? Is the world topsy-turvy?" Johnson wondered. When he regained his composure, he blamed "outside agitators who moved from city to city making trouble."[89]

President Johnson revealed his fear that blacks would behave as he believed they did in Congress during Reconstruction when they "ran into the chamber with bare feet and white women" and "were simply not prepared for their responsibility."[90] Illustrating that his earlier racial beliefs had not changed, he worried that "Negroes will end up [urinating] in the aisles of the Senate."[91]

During the Johnson administration, African-Americans benefited from the enactment of dozens of social programs including Model Cities, urban transportation, child nutrition, anti-poverty, education, and other programs of the Great Society.[92] Educational programs were particularly important, including the Upward Bound program, which allowed low-income and minority youth who had been accepted into colleges to attend summer sessions and thereby bolster their chances of academic success.[93] These and other educational programs helped increase black college enrollment from 270,000 in 1965 to 1.1 million in 1977.[94]

President Johnson was not about to be seen as soft on black violence, so he condemned black rioters even as he offered programs designed to restore domestic tranquility.[95] On a broader level, Johnson continued to allow J. Edgar Hoover's FBI to conduct counter-insurgency intelligence operations, including the infamous COINTELPRO program, on black organizations.

BLACK REBELLION
AND WHITE BACKLASH

After dozens of disorders in African-American ghettos in 1966, the following year witnessed an explosion of spontaneous eruptions of rioting. Detroit, Newark, Atlanta, Cincinnati, and scores of other cities were engulfed by black looting, arson, and, often, sniping. Detroit experienced the most massive and widespread disorder. More than 7,200 people were arrested, and 43 people were killed in violence that involved gun battles between police and elusive snipers.[96] During the Detroit riot, President Johnson asked J. Edgar Hoover to search for a "central character" and "central theme" to the urban rebellions.[97]

Johnson's 1968 decision not to run for reelection resulted from a profound demoralization with the course of his presidency.[98] Following the February 1968 Tet Offensive in Vietnam, enthusiasm for the American intervention ebbed, while domestic turmoil roiled the nation. President Johnson's decision was followed by the assassination of Martin Luther King in Memphis on April 4, 1968, and the accompanying black rebellions.

A scene from the 1966 riots that rocked the nation

CHAPTER SIX

THE POST-CIVIL RIGHTS ERA AND THE AMERICAN PRESIDENTS

RICHARD NIXON AND AFRICAN-AMERICANS

Recast and reinvigorated, Richard M. Nixon looked toward 1968 with a new determination and confidence. Following his crushing defeat in the race for governor of California in 1962, Nixon benefited from the lessons of his Republican electoral defeats in 1960 and 1964.[1] While never a racial liberal, adhering to a middle-of-the-road position between being an advocate of civil rights and a segregationist, Nixon watched the success of Alabama Governor George Wallace with considerable interest. More conscious of the political reality of race and racism than ever, he would utilize them as blunt instruments in carefully formulating strategies and tactics to defeat his Democratic opponents. Being neutral on civil rights had cost him the election in 1960 as he had failed to win anti-black white votes and as well as black votes.[2]

The years of Spiro Agnew (left) and Richard Nixon proved to be a setback for African-Americans.

Born in 1913 in Yorba Linda, California, Nixon was raised in modest circumstances. Following his undergraduate years at Whittier, Nixon enrolled in Duke University Law School in 1934. This experience in the South led him to feel "strongly that it was time to bring the South back into the Union."[3] By 1950, he was elected to the United States Senate. Nixon supported the 1957 Civil Rights Bill, while at the same time he chaired the president's committee on eliminating racial discrimination in firms that contracted with the federal government.[4]

The 1968 election featured, in effect, George Wallace offering white voters a "rollback" of black gains and Richard Nixon offering a "containment" and then a rollback of these advances.[5] Democratic presidential nominee, Senator Hubert H. Humphrey of Minnesota, tried to downplay his liberalism and to appear tough on crime.[6] Repeatedly, he used the phrase "law and order" and only later did he discuss subjects that reflected black interests.[7]

During the campaign, Nixon attacked social programs that had yielded only "an ugly harvest of frustrations, violence and failure across the land."[8] To substitute for these programs, Nixon would use tax and credit policy reforms and use the natural mechanisms of the free enterprise system to facilitate black progress.[9] "Black Americans—no more than white Americans—do not want more Government programs which perpetuate dependency. They don't want to be a colony in a nation."[10] Daniel P. Moynihan's *The Negro Family*, published in 1965 to a firestorm of controversy, was relied upon by Nixon. Soon Moynihan recommended "benign neglect" of blacks in favor of other minorities. This recommendation was greeted by Nixon's enthusiastic response, "I agree!"[11]

One key element of Nixon's southern strategy was set in place following a June 1, 1968, meeting in Atlanta with Senator Strom Thurmond of South Carolina. Nixon promised to allow Thurmond to veto his vice-presidential choice and, most important, committed himself to finding a way not to enforce desegregation, especially school desegregation, if Thurmond would influence the southern Republican delegates to support him at the convention.[12] Subsequently, Nixon made known his opposition to busing, open housing, and other African-American interests.[13] This stance was particularly important for Nixon's prospects of victory since George Wallace appeared on the ballots of every state and threatened to siphon important votes away from Nixon especially in the South.

SPIRO T. AGNEW AND
THE POLITICS OF RACE

Nixon's choice of Spiro Agnew as his vice-presidential running mate constituted a key aspect of his southern strategy. Spiro Theodore Agnew was born in November of 1918 in downtown Baltimore, Maryland, to an upwardly mobile Greek-American family. Following Martin Luther King's assassination, Baltimore—like scores of other cities and towns—experienced an African-American rebellion.[14] Agnew was outraged at the outbreak of lawlessness in his hometown. He called a meeting with the principal black leaders of Baltimore while the army was still pacifying the city. Flanked by these high-ranking military and police officers within a city still occupied by the army, Agnew delivered his terse statement. He denounced black leadership for not preventing the burning and looting of the city by speaking out, causing his audience to walk out before he could finish the speech. Terming them "circuit-riding, Hanoi-visiting . . . caterwauling, riot-inciting, burn-America-down type of leader[s]," Agnew accused them of "breaking and running" when they should have been on the streets stopping the riots. One of those who left said that Governor Agnew was "as sick as any bigot in America."[15]

This and similar acts earned Agnew a national reputation. For Richard M. Nixon, the leading Republican presidential hopeful who was bound to choose a running mate acceptable to Strom Thurmond, this made Spiro T. Agnew an ideal candidate for vice president. Aiming to capture voters attracted by the openly racist message of Alabama's George Wallace, Agnew carried his message to every corner of the nation, fanning the flames of racial resentment.

Immediately after Nixon's victory in the November 1968 presidential election, five southern school districts were threatened with the cutoff of federal funds due to noncompliance with provisions of Title VI of the Civil Rights Act. Southern officials fearing cutoff contacted the team of President-Elect Nixon. They were assured that no cutoff would take place as the Nixon administration would act to postpone the cutoff dates.[16] This was an early signal that the Nixon administration would make good on its promise to retreat on civil rights.

On October 29, 1969, the Supreme Court ruled that the period of "all deliberate speed" in integrating the nation's schools had expired and it was the time for an immediate desegregation of every school district.[17] Having had the opposite intentions, the Nixon administration was stunned by the ruling. Attorney General John Mitchell had earlier expressed the hope that "the Court would respect the administration's wishes" for another postponement in desegregation of southern school districts. Nixon announced his support for an amendment by Senator John Stennis of Mississippi that mandated a uniform enforcement of desegregation decrees in both northern and southern districts. This aimed to delay and cloud the issue by forcing northern whites to experience the "pain" of desegregation along with southern whites.[18]

Leon Panetta of the Department of Health, Education, and Welfare (HEW) was sacked and replaced by Robert C. Mardian, notably more sympathetic to the opponents of desegregation and black civil rights.[19] In one interview, HEW's Robert Finch indicated that "separate but really equal schools" were acceptable to him provided it was voluntary and there was "no evidence of any intimidation of any kind."[20] Finch argued that "it's totally artificial to insist on busing schoolchildren," further gratifying the Nixon white constituency who were fearful of integration in the North.[21]

By the summer of 1970, President Nixon told his advisers to "quit bragging about school desegregation. We do what the law requires—nothing more."[22] He didn't want any members of his administration "praising 'our great record.'"[23] Nixon coldly reasoned that "we will get no credit from blacks but a lot of heat from our own supporters." He ordered his aides to give "as low a profile as possible" on desegregation. He directed his subordinates to oppose busing "at every opportunity."[24] By 1971, Nixon was calling for Congress to mandate a "moratorium" on busing for racial balance. The president proposed the Equal Educational Opportunities Act of 1972, a policy designed to "improve" black education without busing.[25]

NIXON'S WAR ON THE AFRICAN-AMERICAN COMMUNITY

The initial years of Nixon's presidency were marked by an unrelenting repression of radical and not-so-radical black political organizations and movements. Nixon was aided in this endeavor by the FBI, which had already in progress a massive surveillance campaign of black community groups, leaders, and rank-and-file participants. In August 1967, the FBI initiated a new effort that encompassed the wide spectrum of black community activities within its broad scope. Nonviolent civil rights groups, "Black Power" groups, and revolutionary organizations—violent or nonviolent—were targeted by these surveillance activities that grouped them under the label "Black Hate Groups."[26] By October 1967, the "Ghetto Listening Post" and "Ghetto Informant" programs were initiated.[27] Key institutions, enterprises, and areas of the community were targeted in an effort to recruit storeowners, bartenders, veterans, taxi drivers, and others to provide detailed intelligence information to the government.[28] By the early 1970s, every meeting in African-American communities nationwide was within the potential scope of the federal, state, and local intelligence agencies. The most active organizations, of virtually every political stripe, were being monitored clandestinely.[29]

The COINTELPRO program went considerably farther than merely collecting data on black community activities. Its goals were to "expose, disrupt, misdirect, discredit, or otherwise neutralize the activities of black nationalist, hate-type organizations and groupings, their leadership, spokesmen, membership, and supporters." This would have the long-term impact of stunting the organizations' development and miring them in mutual hostility and internal conflict.[30]

The FBI extensively harassed particular groups such as the Black Panther Party and the Revolutionary Action Movement (RAM). Often police would cooperate in making repeated arrests of activists, leaving them financially exhausted, incarcerated, or demoralized.[31] In 1969, the Black Panthers bore the brunt of this escalating onslaught with more than 348 members arrested on a variety of serious charges. On several occasions, police and federal agents laid siege to their offices, leading to prolonged shootouts. The FBI most feared the Panthers' suc-

The Black Panthers were seen by the FBI to be a threat.

cessful development of community-based social programs, such as the Free Breakfast for Children Program. William C. Sullivan of the FBI ordered his subordinates: "Eradicate [the Panthers'] 'serve the people' programs."[32] By the middle of 1969, the FBI was operating against more than 42 Panther chapters and more than 1,200 members.[33] By the end of the Johnson administration, the FBI had an estimated 3,300 "racial ghetto-type informants," in the bureau's terminology. But by the end of Nixon's first administration, the estimate had more than doubled, totaling 7,500. The policy of the FBI was "to thoroughly saturate every level of activity in the ghetto."[34]

PRESIDENT GERALD FORD AND AFRICAN-AMERICANS

On October 12, 1973, following the resignation of Vice President Spiro T. Agnew due to pending federal charges of income tax evasion, Gerald Ford was sworn in as his successor. Nixon reasoned that Ford's appointment would help him conciliate Congress and, due to Ford's relative low stature, make it virtually inconceivable that Nixon would be impeached.[35] Yet, the unthinkable happened as the Watergate scandal deepened, culminating in the August 1974 resignation of President Richard M. Nixon.

After taking office, President Ford followed in the previous administration's footsteps. Two months after becoming president, Ford supported Boston whites who were battling against court-ordered busing.[36] Gerald Ford was a determined foe of busing, carefully crafting a stance designed to win over a large portion of the white electorate. In May 1976, Ford ordered his attorney general to find a test case on busing for school desegregation.[37] At the same time, Ford defended the right of parents to educate their children at segregated academies.[38] In June 1976, President Ford sent legislation to Congress designed to "safeguard domestic tranquility and the future of American education" by limiting busing. The NAACP's Roy Wilkins attacked this move as a "craven, cowardly, despicable retreat."[39]

President Ford cultivated anti-black racial sentiment in his effort to get reelected. He was largely successful in this endeavor, losing only narrowly to Governor Jimmy Carter of Georgia.

PRESIDENT JIMMY CARTER AND AFRICAN-AMERICAN DISILLUSIONMENT

"Please vote for me, vote for open doors," shouted Reverend Clennon King, a 55-year-old African-American, speaking to President-Elect Jimmy Carter as he entered the Plains Baptist Church that Sunday. Only twelve days prior, Carter's narrow victory over Republican incumbent President Gerald Ford was realized through massive black electoral support. Now, due to an unexpected controversy, an embarrassed Carter was unable to savor his victory and quietly formulate plans for his new administration. At issue was the whites-only policy of the church within which he enjoyed the status of being a deacon and its most famous member. In the 11th hour, a controversy over racism threatened the Carter campaign. Under fire, Carter desperately attempted to separate his views from those of the church. "Anyone who lives in our community and who wants to be a member of our church, regardless of race, ought to be admitted," he said. Clearly, he did not resign from the church, for that would have risked incurring the wrath of his white constituency, who would punish any such buckling under to black demands.

Unfortunately for Carter, Clennon King was determined. "Don't you tell me these doors aren't going to open," the African-American minister declared. "They're going to open."[40] The president-elect reiterated his support for allowing blacks to become members, but he insisted that King was not fit for membership. He declared that "King is here to disrupt the church. His brother knows it. The blacks know it. We know it. He's crazy. I could not vote for this man under these circumstances, and I don't think anyone else could either."[41] Carter pressured his resistant fellow townsfolk, arguing that the "world is looking at this church."[42] Therefore, Carter was relieved and "proud" of his church after they voted 120 to 66 to open membership to blacks.[43] Nevertheless, they angrily rejected Reverend Clennon King's application for membership.[44]

Born on October 1, 1924, James Earl Carter, Jr., grew up in a plantation environment of black oppression and white supremacy. When Jimmy was four, his father, Earl, moved the family to a farm home adjacent to an African-American community.[45] Earl's "magic" with money often seemed to involve the labor and business of the neighboring blacks. His land of 4,000 acres (1,600 ha), in different sites, was worked by more than 200

President Carter (right) meeting with Jesse Jackson

black sharecroppers. They labored on "Mr. Earl's" land for one dollar a day for men, seventy-five cents for women, and a quarter for children.[46] It was a long day, beginning before sunrise until after sunset.

The young Jimmy Carter thrived from an early age in this social environment. While still a youth, Carter bought five black tenant shacks. The young Carter's real estate yielded him $16.50 per month in rental income during that period.[47] Then, in 1962, Carter began serving in the Georgia State Senate; in 1966, Carter ran for governor and lost. His eventual electoral victory was achieved after a refashioning of his image as a racial liberal.[48]

But, in a tradition reaching back to the old slaveholding presidents, Carter continued to profit from the labor of his black employees who, until he became a presidential candidate, continued to receive less than white workers for the same tasks.[49] During the presidential campaign, Carter said that he saw "nothing wrong with ethnic purity being maintained." He indicated that he "would not force the racial integration of a neighborhood by government action," while he would still prohibit housing discrimination.[50]

On February 3, 1977, roughly two weeks after he took office, President Carter met with a group of black leaders. Not only was the number of black appointees in his administration at issue, but so was the poor funding of programs to reduce teenage unemployment.[51] Despite the dissatisfaction of African-Americans with the number of appointees, there were a few highly publicized black appointments. Notably, Patricia Roberts Harris was named as secretary of the Department of Housing and Urban Development (HUD), Andrew Young was named the United Nations special ambassador, Wade McCree was appointed solicitor general, Clifford Alexander as secretary of the Army, and John Slaughter as chairman of the National Science Foundation.[52] However, the appointment of Griffin

Bell of Georgia as attorney general was regarded as another sign of the shortcomings of the young Carter administration. Bell was a member of whites-only clubs, a former supporter of Carswell for the Supreme Court, and a judicial defender of segregated institutions. His appointment conformed disturbingly to the patterns of previous administrations.[53]

Andrew Young was named special ambassador to the United Nations during the Carter administration.

In May 1977, the Carter administration announced that there would be no new social welfare, health, and educational initiatives.[54] The promise to drastically cut the defense budget was similarly forgotten. The 1978 Carter budget proposed cutbacks in social programs, incurring the wrath of more liberal politicians. By August 1977, key black leaders who had supported Carter's campaign—including Jesse Jackson, Vernon Jordan, and Benjamin Hooks—charged President Carter with "callous neglect," declaring that the Carter administration had "betrayed" black America.[55]

Vernon Jordan, in particular, was harshly critical of President Carter. Speaking to the 67th annual meeting of the Urban League, Jordan declared to his audience that "black people and poor people . . . resent unfulfilled promises of jobs, compromises to win conservative support and the continued acceptance of high unemployment."[56]

Columnist Chuck Stone was particularly critical of Carter's "paternalistic racism" and "political ineptitude." He noted that instead of implementing his campaign promises, Carter substituted symbolism, such as appearing at a black church on Sunday morning.[57]

High on the agenda of African-American leadership was the Humphrey-Hawkins bill that would provide radical measures to alleviate the increasingly acute unemployment problems endured by African-Americans.[58] Carter failed to push aggressively for the bill, since he was more concerned with attempting to reach a balanced budget and with broadening his support beyond the traditional Democratic constituency.

THE 1980 PRESIDENTIAL CAMPAIGN: A TURNING POINT FOR BLACK AMERICA

Presidential candidate Ronald Reagan skillfully played to his white southern audiences. Reagan chose Philadelphia, Mississippi, to kick off his 1980 campaign, a town remembered principally for the 1964 slayings of three civil rights workers. Later during the campaign, in Neshoba, Mississippi, Reagan told a crowd of white segregationist supporters that he felt strongly about "states' rights."[59] His target constituency was clear.

Nancy Reagan once said to her husband, unaware her telephone call was being amplified, "I wish you could be here to see all these beautiful white people." Her comment clearly indicated the deliberate cultivation of a white constituency, based on appeal to their base anti-black prejudices.[60] Reagan's priority target groups included southern whites, northern working-class whites, white ethnic group members, and conservative white rural residents.[61]

In the 1980 election, African-American leadership, as well as the overwhelming proportion of the black population, faced the familiar dilemma of choosing between two candidates that could be generously described as less than perfect. It was yet another case of choosing between the "lesser of two evils." Not surprisingly, despite the disappointment with Carter, most black leaders endorsed his reelection.

On the eve of the election, Jesse Jackson authored an op-ed feature for *The Atlanta Constitution,* urging a vote for Jimmy Carter. Jackson argued that the Carter administration "has supported the enforcement of existing civil rights laws" and, in his campaign, has rejected the use of "racial code words such as 'law and order' or 'busing' to divide the America people" as Reagan had done. Jackson also praised the appointment of more than "50 members of minority groups to federal judgeships," which was more than all previous presidents combined.[62]

Reagan won the 1980 presidential election handily, winning 43,899,248 votes, or 50.75 percent, to Carter's 35,481,435, or 41.02 percent of the total vote.[63] Significantly, Carter received 90 percent of the African-American vote, while Reagan obtained 56 percent of the white vote.

PRESIDENT REAGAN AND THE POST–CIVIL RIGHTS ERA

Taking a break during a roast with veteran black journalist Carl Rowan, President Ronald Reagan lamented that he had been misunderstood "on this business of racism." Reagan said, "I tried hard to win friendship among blacks, but couldn't do it. I talked to black leaders after my election in 1980, and they went out and criticized me in horrible ways." For this, Reagan admitted, he said, "to hell with 'em."[64]

President Ronald Reagan's policies toward black America were clearly not solely the result of a post-election chill. For three decades, Reagan's politics cultivated a conservatism marked by a distinct strain of hostility toward blacks and their advance in American society. Indeed, Reagan as president did more than merely say "to hell with 'em," taking a proactive role in rolling back civil rights and black progress. In terms of the administration's direct and clearly visible actions against African-American interests, one would have to go back to the

Democratic administration of Woodrow Wilson to find parallels. For black America, the Reagan era proved to be a stern test of the strength and maturity of its political institutions after decades of growth. Ultimately, the Reagan challenge led to the creation of a new form of independent black politics: the emergence of the Rainbow Coalition and Jesse Jackson.

Ronald Wilson Reagan was born in February 1911 in Illinois. The future president grew up in small-town America in an atmosphere that later allowed him to state that during his youth there was not a "black problem." In his autobiography, however, Reagan recalls that at the "local movie theater, blacks and whites had to sit apart—the blacks in the balcony.[65] According to Ronald Reagan, his father imbued him with a hatred of racists and racism. He recalled when the historic movie *Birth of a Nation* was shown in his hometown, "My brother and I were the only kids not to see it," Reagan said. His father then explained, according to Reagan, that the movie "deals with the Ku Klux Klan against the colored folks, and I'm damned if anyone in this family will go see it."[66]

THE REAGAN PRESIDENCY: AN ASSAULT ON BLACK AMERICA

In 1981, while addressing the annual NAACP convention, President Ronald Reagan boldly asserted that liberal bureaucrats in Washington had made "needy people government dependent, rather than independent." Reagan described this as a new variety of "bondage," declaring that in the same manner "as the Emancipation Proclamation freed black people 118 years ago, today we need to declare an economic emancipation," implying that "welfare" and other social programs had enslaved black America.

On another occasion, Reagan told African-American clergy "it's better to create jobs by restoring the economy than to provide handouts. Some well-meaning [government] programs robbed recipients of their dignity, trapped them into a dependency that left them with idle time, less self-respect, and little prospect of a better future."[67] In Reagan's 1982 State of the Union message, he proposed to create "urban enterprise zones." The "broad range of special economic incentives" to foster economic development would include minimum- and sub-minimum-wage labor in impoverished areas.[68]

Upon taking office, President Reagan immediately embarked upon fulfilling his pledge to cut scores of social programs. Programs involving welfare, housing aid, mass transit, student assistance, and medical care suffered drastic cutbacks.[69] Almost immediately, the impact of Reagan's election was felt in many low-income and African-American communities.

THE REAGAN ADMINISTRATION AND CIVIL RIGHTS

Reagan, with great reluctance, announced his support in 1982 of a ten-year extension of the Voting Rights Act. Attempting to counter the growing chorus of critics of his civil rights policies, Reagan included a firm statement on civil rights in his 1982 State of the Union message.[70]

Yet, from the beginning of the Reagan administration, civil rights enforcement was weakened. President Reagan and his first attorney general, William French Smith, fought to change the Internal Revenue Service policy that forbade tax exemptions to racially discriminatory private educational institutions. In January 1982, the Justice Department asked the Supreme Court to dismiss lawsuits against North Carolina and South Carolina private schools that were in immediate danger of losing their tax exemptions. This act fulfilled one of Reagan's campaign pledges to his southern and anti-black constituency.[71]

Clarence Pendleton, Jr., was named by President Ronald Reagan to be head of the U.S. Commission on Civil Rights.

The appointment of William Bradford Reynolds III as the Reagan administration's head of the Civil Rights Division of the Justice Department—as well as the appointment of Clarence Pendleton, Jr., as the head of the U.S. Commission on Civil Rights—served to temper the hopes of anyone clinging to any possibility that Reagan would be more liberal on civil rights than his campaign rhetoric indicated.[72] Both men served as the point men of the Reagan administration on civil rights issues. While Pendleton was African-American and Reynolds a wealthy white heir to the Du Pont fortune, both led a concerted push by the Reagan administration to roll back the civil rights gains of the previous decades. Reynolds became a symbol of the Reagan administration's pursuit of policies aimed at weakening black voting rights, destroying affirmative action programs, halting busing, preventing desegregation, and undermining the U.S. Civil Rights Commission.

In March 1985, the Reagan administration sued the District of Columbia, charging that the affirmative action plan of its fire department granted discriminatory preferences "based on race and sex." Ronald L. Ellis, a NAACP Legal Defense and Education Fund attorney called it a "sad day" that the Justice Department found itself on the side of those actively fighting attempts to end discrimination. Ellis concluded that the Reagan administration's lawsuit was "consistent with the administration's pattern of trying to roll back the calendar" in the fight against racism.[73]

Another Reagan African-American appointee, Samuel R. Pierce, as secretary of the Department of Housing and Urban Development (HUD), oversaw huge budget cuts in low-income housing—from $33 billion in 1982 to only $8 billion in 1988. Staff cuts disrupted the agency's structure. Whole divisions were removed, key positions remained unfilled, and review committees were ignored as top staffers increasingly made arbitrary decisions.

When President Reagan then nominated Judge Robert Bork to the U.S. Supreme Court, it triggered a full-scale mobilization of liberals, minorities, labor, and women in an attempt to prevent his confirmation. Judge Bork's past decisions and interpretations of the Constitution alarmed a broad swath of the public, ultimately leading to his rejection by the Senate with a vote of 58 to 42. Many regarded this rejection as the most important setback for Reagan and Reaganism since his triumphant victory over incumbent Jimmy Carter.[74]

President Reagan's already abysmally low popularity rating among African-Americans fell even further from 14 percent in September 1981 to 8 percent in 1982.[75] By mid-1983, the chorus of African-Americans critical of Reagan was deafening. Not only had tens of thousands of blacks lost government positions following Reagan's ascension to the presidency, but also his opposition to affirmative action served to chill the atmosphere with respect to the hiring of blacks. Reagan set an example at the top by appointing few blacks. Whereas 12 percent of President Carter's appointments were black, only 4.1 percent of Reagan's were.[76] While Carter appointed 38 African-American judges of the 262 he named, Reagan appointed only 7 of the 385 he named.[77]

Reagan's impact could be especially felt as a $1 billion cut in Medicaid and the elimination of more than a million Aid to

Families with Dependent Children (AFDC) recipients shredded the fabric of millions of lives. Immediately, a marked increase in beggars, homeless, and mentally impaired people could be seen on the streets of major American cities.

AFRICAN-AMERICAN ELECTORAL INSURGENCY: THE JACKSON REVOLUTION

Jesse Jackson, beset by generally negative media coverage, ran an inspiring race with a program that mocked the bland, business-as-usual approach of the traditional presidential candidates. African-Americans, having been locked out of any consideration whatsoever for most of U.S. history, were never considered for the presidency. Jesse Jackson's performance—on the campaign trail, in the debates, and at the podium—was, in one sense, the historical vindication of the decades of slander and

Jesse Jackson's campaigns for the presidency brought hope to African-Americans.

abuse hurled at the African-Americans. Jackson's candidacy inspired new levels of political activism, manifested in many new candidacies for lesser offices in African-American communities across the nation. Although in 1984 and in 1988, Jackson's primary victories represented the interests of a broader segment of America than African-Americans, in a very real way he became the personification of black political interests. Indeed, the Jackson platform reflected the long-sought-after goals of African-Americans. "What does Jesse Jackson really want?" was a question that traditional pundits posed repeatedly, overlapping with the underlying question of "What does black America want?"

The wildly successful campaign of Jesse Jackson in the 1984 Democratic Party primaries upset the balance of American politics. The Jackson quest for the presidency was greeted by an unprecedented level of enthusiasm from African-Americans, particularly those of the lower socioeconomic strata.[78] In the end, Jackson finished third in the campaign for the Democratic nomination for president. However, the longer-term implication of the 1984 campaign, by mobilizing voters for Jackson, influenced senate races in Illinois, Tennessee, and other states, thereby preparing the way for the defeat of Reagan's Supreme Court nominee Judge Robert Bork.[79]

In 1984, Jackson enhanced his international image as the "president of black America" by putting forth, in effect, an alternative African-American foreign policy perspective. Traveling to Cuba, he defied American policy-makers by embracing Cuban leader Fidel Castro. Jackson's efforts in this arena suggest an assertive African-American approach to foreign policy, buttressing the black institutions that had gradually developed over the course of the previous two decades, including Transafrica and the Congressional Black Caucus (CBC).

The dramatic release of U.S. Navy pilot Lieutenant Robert Goodman provided a boost for the credibility of the Jackson campaign. Jackson confidently went to "rescue" Goodman, after many African-Americans became concerned that the Reagan administration was not taking an active interest in securing the release of the downed African-American pilot. Later, traveling to the blockaded nation of Cuba, Jackson met with President Fidel Castro and accompanied him to church, the first time the Cuban leader had been to church in seventeen years.[80] In January 1984, an embarrassed President Ronald Reagan grudgingly met with Jesse Jackson and the freed Lieutenant Robert Goodman at the White House.

In January 1984 Jackson made remarks that referred to New York City as "Hymietown" (a derogatory term for Jewish people). When these comments became known to the public, it proved to be a persistent problem for his candidacy. The ignoring of Jackson's request for an off-the-record discussion with *Washington Post* reporter Milton Coleman, an African-American, led to the revelation that Jackson had slandered Jews in private.[81] In late February 1984, Jesse Jackson formally apologized for his remarks before an assembly of Jewish Americans at a Jewish synagogue in New Hampshire.[82]

Four years later, the new 1988 Super Tuesday election day, which featured twenty races across the South, was the setting for a stunning triumph by the Jackson-led forces. Jackson won a total of 91 percent of the African-American vote and the most popular votes of any candidate on Super Tuesday.[83] The momentum of the Jackson campaign continued with strong showings in several states including Illinois and Michigan. The 1988 campaign culminated in Jackson's moving speech at the Democratic National Convention. Eyes grew moist as Jackson hammered home his themes in the powerful oratorical tradition of the African-American minister-politician. Jackson recounted how he himself was "born to a teenage mother" who "was not supposed to make it."

I wasn't born in the hospital. Mama didn't have insurance. I was born in the bed at home. I really do understand. Born in a three-room house, bathroom in the backyard, slop jar by the bed, no hot and cold running water. I understand. Wallpaper used for decoration? No. For a windbreaker. I understand. . . .[84]

While Governor Michael Dukakis of Massachusetts won the Democratic nomination, African-American communities resonated with Jackson's admonition to "keep hope alive." After all, testifying to the character of African-Americans, "suffering breeds character," "character breeds faith," and ultimately, "faith will not disappoint."[85] As Jackson so eloquently said, in his address to the 1988 Democratic National Convention

You must not surrender. You may or may not get there, but just know that you're qualified and you hold on and hold out. We must never surrender. America will get better and better. Keep hope alive. Keep hope alive. Keep hope alive.[86]

GEORGE BUSH, WILLIE HORTON, AND AFRICAN-AMERICAN PROGRESS

By 1988, black Americans were mired in a frustration borne from having suffered through two terms of Ronald Reagan, one term of Jimmy Carter, and the terms of Nixon and Ford. African-American social and economic progress had stagnated and, in many areas, experienced reverses. While the overall socioeconomic environment surrounding African-Americans had improved since World War II—making possible widespread, if circumscribed and limited, financial gains—barriers to upward black social mobility had increased. For the black middle class as a whole, the relative improvement compared to that of the white counterparts has been limited. In 1978, the percentage of black-to-white per capita income peaked at 59.4 percent. By 1987, this percentage had fallen to 57.5 percent. By 1987, black family income stood at only 56.1 percent of white family income.[87]

Within the context of an increasingly collective self-perception of the black community as in crisis, Vice President George H. W. Bush discovered the political utility of racial symbols and code words. "Willie Horton" was used as a symbol of African-Americans and African-American interests. High wages, social programs, and inflation were all subtly captured by the general focus on Horton. The focus on Horton's real crimes could serve as a symbolic introduction to the politics of liberalism and the implied appeasement of black Americans. Willie Horton was a media creation that grew from the actual William Horton, a convicted murderer who in April 1987 raped a white woman after tying up her fiancé and then stealing his car. Bush connected this heinous act to the Massachusetts furlough program from which Horton had escaped. In speech after speech, Bush and Republican campaigners hammered away at this theme, tying Democratic nominee Michael Dukakis with Horton and with crime. This connection to other African-Americans and "liberal" and black issues and interests was unmistakable. The Republican support group "Americans for Bush" paid for the Horton ads and a national tour for Horton's victims.[88]

This strategy was the brainchild of Lee Atwater, a southern-born Republican strategist who had no qualms about appealing to the rawest racial prejudices of white Americans. Atwater eagerly anticipated confronting Dukakis with the constant image of Horton, especially before southern white audiences, who were viewed as the key constituency in a Republican victory. To the extent that Dukakis was forced to give respect to the figure of Jesse Jackson, Atwater sought to exploit this fact and win votes for George Bush.[89] On his deathbed, Atwater later apologized to William Horton, Jr., for vilifying him.[90]

THE BUSH ADMINISTRATION AND AFRICAN-AMERICANS

Aside from President Bush's nomination of Clarence Thomas for the Supreme Court, the appointment of Colin Powell as chairman of the Joint Chiefs of Staff was the most important African-American appointment. Constance Newman was appointed the head of the Office of Personnel Management, and Louis Sullivan became secretary of the Department of Health and Human Services.

Powell's appointment represented perhaps the most powerful position an African-American has ever occupied in the history of the United States and, despite its questionable significance in terms of black political power, signified a new stage in relationships between black appointees and chief executives. The inclusion of Powell in heretofore closed corners of American policy-making marked a new level of inclusiveness of the American political elite, heralding new opportunities for African-Americans amenable to the political establishment.

General Colin Powell was named by President George Bush as chairman of the Joint Chiefs of Staff.

THE DRUG WAR AGAINST
BLACK AMERICA

Lured by agents of President George Bush to Lafayette Park, across from the White House, Keith Jackson, an African-American teenager, was used to demonstrate the pervasiveness of drugs in the nation.[91] Taking advantage of a heightened national concern about the spread of drugs and crime, and spurred by the upsurge of crack cocaine addiction, George Bush sought to maintain a political momentum by once again using a black criminal to mobilize his constituency. Bush's general in his war was William J. Bennett, the National Drug Policy director, or "drug czar." Contemptuous of underlying causes of drug usage and crime, Bennett led the fight for a massive expansion of the nation's prison system and for tougher penalties for all categories of drug offenses, while virtually ignoring the need for more drug treatment programs. Bennett's emergency plan for the District of Columbia relied heavily on the expansion of prison space and devoted only 5 percent of its budget to treatment and education.[92] Under the Bush administration's Bennett, the inequities of the fight against drugs became even more graphic. While African-Americans were only roughly 12 percent of the users of illegal drugs, they represented 41 percent of those arrested on cocaine or heroin charges.[93]

THE SUPREME COURT NOMINATION
OF CLARENCE THOMAS

In late 1991, the nomination of Clarence Thomas to the U.S. Supreme Court caused even more than the considerable amount of controversy that had been anticipated. Initially, the Senate Judiciary Committee hearings for the former head of the Equal Employment Opportunities Commission (EEOC) had gone smoothly. Sailing toward his confirmation, Thomas was suddenly faced with charges that he sexually harassed black attorney Anita Hill during his tenure at the EEOC. The stunned 43-year-old Thomas vehemently denied harassment had occurred, and the nation became embroiled in a new level of debate over the issue of sexual harassment in the workplace.

From the beginning, the Black Caucus opposed the nomination of Thomas, and it worked quietly to block his confirmation.[94] Representative Major R. Owen (D-NY) termed Thomas a "monstrous negative role model" and a "Benedict Arnold." He went on to say, "The elevation of this man to the Supreme Court would be a gross insult, a slap in the face of all African-Americans."[95] Ultimately, Clarence Thomas, pushed to his limit, declared himself to be the victim of a "high-tech lynching," as he and President Bush allied to cry racism at those who opposed his nomination. While Thomas was eventually confirmed, victory was costly for President Bush, who lost support among women and blacks.[96]

President George Bush (right) with Supreme Court nominee Clarence Thomas

THE CLINTON ADMINISTRATION

In the 1992 presidential election, William Jefferson Clinton received 43 percent of the vote, defeating George Bush, who received 39 percent. Once again, African-American hopes were raised by the prospect of a return to the somewhat mythical era of a Democratic administration. Only a few remembered that previous Democratic administrations—Roosevelt's, Truman's, Kennedy's, and Carter's—were marked by an inertia broken only by the aggressive thrust of the black drive for freedom. However, during the Clinton campaign for the presidency, there were strong hints that his approach to winning and maintaining African-American support would be different. He seemed to respond to the widespread perception that the campaign of Michael Dukakis was ruined by the impression that Jesse Jackson and blacks played an important role in the direction of the Democratic Party. A deliberate snub of Jackson at a meeting of his own Rainbow Coalition—by attacking intemperate statements by rapper Sista Souljah—successfully distanced Bill Clinton from Jesse Jackson and the African-Americans.[97]

President Bill Clinton (right), speaking with Jesse Jackson, made substantial efforts to improve race relations.

President Bill Clinton's administration was marked by lofty rhetoric and moving symbolism on race, which were unmatched by policy measures that attacked the most pressing problems facing African-Americans. During the early years of his presidency, Clinton pushed through a welfare reform bill and a crime bill, both with ominous implications for African-Americans, especially youth.[98] Despite studies indicating that many impoverished women receiving public assistance would suffer if the proposed legislation to "end welfare as we know it" was passed, the administration nevertheless went forward with it.[99] Ignoring the tremendous growth in numbers of incarcerated black men and women, mainly jailed for nonviolent offenses related to their relative poverty, Clinton proposed legislation that added to the long list of crimes requiring mandatory sentences. Not surprisingly, the number of African-Americans under criminal justice supervision has continued to rise under the Clinton administration, despite the longest peacetime period of economic growth in American history.

No president, however, has appointed to prominent positions as many African-Americans as has President Clinton. Nor has any president made as many statements affirming the principles of racial equality and justice. Appointing historian John Hope Franklin in 1997 to lead a "great and unprecedented conversation about race," Clinton repeatedly attempted to improve the atmosphere of race in the nation.[100] His persistent use of symbolism and his appearances in black communities, particularly while under the threat of impeachment during the Monica Lewinsky scandal, has maintained his African-American support.

LOOKING TO THE FUTURE

African-Americans and the institution of the presidency have traveled a long way since the era of the slave-owning presidents.

Along this rocky road, strewn with obstacles, progress has been forged—culminating in presidents who heed black political power and adhere, at least formally, to the principles of racial equality and justice. History continues to unfold as we progress into the new millennium, and today's problems confronting the national African-American community will inevitably confront future presidents. Perhaps the future will not be as troubled as the past.

Notes

Chapter One

1. Thomas Jefferson. "Notes on Virginia" in *The Writings of Thomas Jefferson*, volume 2 (Washington, DC: The Thomas Jefferson Memorial Association, 1903), p. 227.
2. Lerone Bennett. *Before the Mayflower: The History of the Negro in America* (Baltimore: Penguin, 1962), pp. 29–32.
3. William Loren Katz. *Breaking the Chains: African-American Slave Resistance* (New York: Atheneum, 1990), p. 6.
4. Ibid., p. 7.
5. Ibid., p. 12.
6. Sidney Kaplan. *The Black Presence in the Era of the American Revolution, 1770–1800* (Washington, DC: National Portrait Gallery, Smithsonian Institute, 1973), p. 11.
7. Ibid., p. 14.
8. Katz, p. 21.
9. Drew R. McCoy. *The Last of the Fathers: James Madison and the Republican Legacy* (New York: Cambridge University Press, 1989), p. 263.
10. Kaplan, p. 61.
11. Malcolm Bell, Jr. *Major Butler's Legacy: Five Generations of a Slaveholding Family* (Athens: The University of Georgia Press, 1987), pp. 32–33.
12. John E. Ferling. *The First of Men: A Life of George Washington* (Knoxville: The University of Tennessee Press, 1988), p. 5.
13. Ibid, p. 3.
14. James Thomas Flexner. *George Washington: Anguish and Farewell 1793–1799* (Boston: Little, Brown, 1972), p.113.
15. Ibid.
16. Ibid.
17. Ibid., p. 114.
18. Ibid.

19. Ibid., p. 69.
20. Ferling, p. 477.
21. Ibid., p. 476.
22. Flexner, p. 434.
23. Ferling, p. 476.
24. Flexner, p. 441.
25. Ferling, p. 122.
26. Ibid.
27. Ibid., p. 433.
28. Ibid., p. 121.
29. Ibid., p. 118–119.
30. Ibid., p. 445.
31. Ibid., p. 446.
32. Kaplan, p. 217.
33. Kaplan, p. 8.
34. Ibid.
35. Paul F. Boller, Jr. *Presidential Campaigns* (New York: Oxford University Press, 1984), p. 11.
36. William W. Freehling. *The Road to Disunion: Secessionists at Bay, 1776–1854*, volume 1 (New York: Oxford University Press, 1990), p. 147.
37. Fawn Brodie. *Thomas Jefferson: An Intimate History* (New York: Norton, 1974), p. 47.
38. Ibid.
39. Gordon Wood, "Jefferson at Home," review of *Jeffersonian Legacies,* edited by Peter S. Onuf, *The New York Review of Books* (May 13, 1993), p. 9.
40. John Chester Miller. *The Wolf by the Ears: Thomas Jefferson and Slavery* (New York: The Free Press, 1977), p. 21.
41. Ibid.
42. Ibid., pp. 25–26.
43. Dumas Malone. *Jefferson and the Ordeal of Liberty*, volume 3 of *Jefferson and His Time* (Boston: Little, Brown, 1962), p. 207.
44. Wood, pp. 8–9.
45. Flexner, p. 447.
46. Ronald Takaki. *Iron Cages: Race and Culture in 19th Century America* (New York: Oxford University Press, 1990), p. 44.
47. Jefferson, volume 2, p. 193.
48. Winthrop D. Jordan. *White Over Black: American Attitudes Toward the Negro, 1550–1812* (Baltimore: Penguin, 1969), pp. 455–459.
49. Brodie, p. 288; John Chester Miller, p. 106.
50. Brodie, p. 350.
51. Jefferson, volume 2, p. 195.
52. Kaplan, p. 120.

53. Kaplan, p. 123.
54. Jefferson, volume 2, p. 196.
55. Kaplan, p. 167.
56. John Chester Miller, p. 218.
57. Ibid, pp. 219–220.
58. Freehling, p. 157.
59. John Chester Miller, p. 273.
60. Robert A. Rutland. *James Madison, the Founding Father* (New York: Macmillan, 1987), p. 10.
61. Jordan, p. 432.
62. Rutland, p. 230.
63. Ibid, p. 261.
64. W. T. Hutchinson and William M. E. Rachal, editors. "To William Bradford" in *The Papers of John Madison*, volume 1 (Chicago: University of Chicago Press, 1962), p. 130.
65. Freehling, pp. 150–152.
66. Melvin H. Buxbaum. *Ben Franklin: A Reference Guide, 1907–1983* (Boston: G. K. Hall, 1988).
67. Eric Foner, editor. *Nat Turner* (Englewood Cliffs, NJ: Prentice-Hall, 1971); Sterling Stuckey. *Slave Culture: Nationalist Theory and the Foundations of Black America* (New York: Oxford University Press, 1987).
68. Bennett, p. 112.
69. Harry Ammon. *James Monroe: The Quest for National Identity* (New York: Scribner, 1971), p. 200.
70. Ibid., p. 187.
71. Ibid., pp. 199–200.
72. Ibid., p. 200.
73. Ibid., p. 199.
74. Freehling, p. 155.
75. McCoy, p. 270.
76. Ammon, pp. 451–52.
77. Freehling, p. 155.
78. Ibid.
79. Herbert Aptheker. *American Negro Slave Revolts* (New York: International Publishers, 1978), p. 270.
80. John Quincy Adams. *The Diary of John Quincy Adams, 1794–1845: American Diplomacy, and Political, Social, and Intellectual Life from Washington to Polk*, edited by Allan Nevins (New York: Scribner, 1951), p. 289.
81. Freehling, p. 155.

CHAPTER TWO

1. Mary W. M. Hargreaves. *The Presidency of John Quincy Adams* (Lawrence: University Press of Kansas, 1985), p. 156.

2. Leonard L. Richards. *The Life and Times of Congressman John Quincy Adams* (New York: Oxford University Press, 1986), p. 14.
3. Hargreaves, p. 156.
4. Richards, pp. 13–14.
5. Ammon, p. 521.
6. Freehling, p. 79.
7. Aptheker, pp. 268–270.
8. Ibid., p. 272.
9. Freehling, p. 254.
10. Richards, pp. 104–105.
11. Ibid., p. 105.
12. Freehling, p. 254.
13. Ibid., p. 257.
14. Richards, p. 75.
15. Freehling, p. 322.
16. Ibid., p. 323.
17. Ibid., p. 324; *see also* Elbert B. Smith. *The Presidencies of Zachary Taylor and Millard Fillmore* (Lawrence: University Press of Kansas, 1988).
18. Jack Shepherd. *The Adams Chronicles: Four Generations of Greatness* (Boston: Little, Brown, 1975), p. 323.
19. Ibid., p. 326.
20. Freehling, pp. 285–286.
21. Ibid., pp. 290–291.
22. J. S. Bassett. *The Life of Andrew Jackson*, volumes 1 and 2 (New York: Archon Books, 1967), pp. 10–11.
23. Ibid., p. 64.
24. Ibid., p. 35.
25. Ibid.
26. Ibid., p. 66)
27. Ibid.; R. V. Remini. *Andrew Jackson and the Course of American Democracy, 1833–1845*, volume III (New York: Harper and Row, 1984), p. xvi.
28. Bassett, p. 157.
29. Ibid.
30. Aptheker, p. 259; Bassett, p. 239.
31. Katz, p. 85.
32. Ibid.
33. Ibid., p. 95.
34. Ibid., pp. 97–98.
35. John Niven. *Martin Van Buren: The Romantic Age of American Politics* (New York: Oxford University Press, 1983), p. 385.
36. Ibid., p. 385.
37. James L. Sundquist. *Dynamics of the Party System: Alignment and*

Realignment of Political Parties in the United States (Washington, DC: The Brookings Institution, 1973), pp. 40–41.

38. Niven, pp. 388–389; Sundquist, p. 41.
39. Robert Seager. *And Tyler Too: A Biography of John and Julia Gardiner Tyler* (New York: McGraw-Hill, 1963), pp. 119–124.
40. Smith. *Zachary Taylor and Millard Fillmore*, p. 31.
41. Freehling, p. 361.
42. Norma Lois Peterson. *The Presidencies of William Henry Harrison and John Tyler* (Lawrence: University Press of Kansas, 1989), p. 19.
43. Seager, p. 53.
44. Ibid.
45. Ibid., p. 103.
46. Ibid., p. 362.
47. Ibid., p. 104.
48. Ibid.
49. Ibid.
50. Paul H. Bergeron. *The Presidency of James Polk* (Lawrence: University Press of Kansas, 1987), p. 9.
51. Charles Sellers. *James K. Polk: Jacksonian, 1795–1843* (Princeton, NJ: Princeton University Press, 1957), p. 108.
52. Ibid., p. 423.
53. Ibid., p. 422.
54. Freehling, p. 492.
55. Smith, *Zachary Taylor and Millard Fillmore*, p. 27.
56. Brainerd Dyer. *Zachary Taylor* (New York: Barnes and Noble, 1956), pp. 72–73.
57. Smith, *Zachary Taylor and Millard Fillmore*, p. 27.
58. Dyer, p. 256.
59. Seager, p. 392.
60. Smith, *Zachary Taylor and Millard Fillmore*, p. 212; James Brewer Stewart. *Wendell Phillips: Liberty's Hero* (Baton Rouge: Louisiana State University, 1986), p. 152.
61. Smith, *Zachary Taylor and Millard Fillmore*, p. 214.
62. Stewart, p. 152.
63. Smith, *Zachary Taylor and Millard Fillmore*, p. 237.
64. Ibid., p. 240.
65. Roy Franklin Nichols. *Franklin Pierce: Young Hickory of Granite Hills* (Norwalk, CT: The Easton Press, 1969), p. 83.
66. Ibid., p. 235.
67. Ibid., p. 361).
68. Stephen B. Oates. *With Malice Toward None: The Life of Abraham Lincoln* (New York: Harper and Row, 1977), pp. 138–139.
69. Elbert B. Smith. *The Presidency of James Buchanan* (Lawrence: University Press of Kansas, 1975), p. 26.

70. Ibid., pp. 26–27.
71. Ibid.; Irving J. Sloan, editor. *James Buchanan, 1791–1868, Chronology—Documents—Bibliographical Aids* (Dobbs Ferry, NY: Oceana Publications, 1968), p. 40.
72. Aptheker, p. 39; Sloan, p. 71.

CHAPTER THREE

1. "The Perpetuation of Our Political Institutions" in *The Speeches of Abraham Lincoln* (New York: The Chesterfield Society, 1908), p. 309; Oates, p. 218.
2. "The Perpetuation of Our Political Institutions," p. 319.
3. Benjamin Quarles. *The Negro in the Civil War* (Boston: Little, Brown, 1969), p. 22.
4. Phillip S. Foner. *The Civil War, 1861–1865*, volume III of *The Life and Writings of Frederick Douglass* (New York: International Publishers, 1952), p. 13.
5. Ibid., p. 17.
6. Ibid., p. 18.
7. Quarles, *The Negro in the Civil War*, p. 148.
8. Ibid., p. 149.
9. Benjamin Quarles. *The Negro in the Making of America* (New York: Macmillan, 1964), p. 114.
10. Phillip S. Foner, *The Civil War*, p. 25.
11. Quarles, *The Negro in the Making of America*, p. 116.
12. Phillip S. Foner, *The Civil War*, p. 46.
13. Ibid., pp. 35–36.
14. Ibid.
15. Ibid., p. 36.
16. Ibid.
17. Oates, p. 38.
18. "The Perpetuation of Our Political Institutions," p. 2.
19. Ibid., p. 4.
20. Oates, p. 85.
21. Ibid., p. 86.
22. "The Perpetuation of Our Political Institutions," p. 52.
23. Smith, *James Buchanan*, p. 28.
24. "The Perpetuation of Our Political Institutions," p. 64.
25. Ibid.
26. Phillip S. Foner, *The Civil War*, pp. 309–319.
27. Ibid., p. 312.
28. Ibid.
29. Ibid.
30. Ibid., p. 314.

31. Eric Foner. *Reconstruction: America's Unfinished Revolution, 1863–1877* (New York: Harper and Row, 1988), p. 113.
32. Ibid., p. 61.
33. Quarles, *The Negro in the Making of America*, p. 117.
34. Eric Foner, *Reconstruction*, p. 223.
35. Leon F. Litwack. *Been in the Storm So Long: The Aftermath of Slavery* (New York: Vintage, 1980), p. 297.
36. Ibid., p. 304.
37. Eric Foner, *Reconstruction*, p. 105.
38. Ibid., pp. 179–180.
39. W. E. B. DuBois. *Black Reconstruction in America* (New York: Atheneum, 1983), pp. 244–245.
40. Ibid., p. 245.
41. Ibid., p. 246.
42. Ibid., p. 247.
43. Albert Castel. *The Presidency of Andrew Johnson* (Lawrence: Regents Press of Kansas, 1979), p. 6.
44. James E. Sefton. *Andrew Johnson and the Uses of Constitutional Power* (Boston: Little, Brown, 1980), p. 22.
45. Eric Foner, *Reconstruction*, p. 107.
46. Sefton, p. 50.
47. Ibid., p. 36.
48. DuBois, *Black Reconstruction in America*, p. 243.
49. Phillip S. Foner. *Reconstruction and After,* volume IV of *The Life and Writings of Frederick Douglass* (New York: International Publishers, 1955), p. 14.
50. DuBois, *Black Reconstruction in America*, p. 263.
51. Ibid., p. 259; Eric Foner, *Reconstruction*, pp. 177–178.
52. Eric Foner, *Reconstruction*, p. 178; DuBois, *Black Reconstruction in America*, pp. 248–249.
53. Castel, p. 63.
54. DuBois, *Black Reconstruction in America*, p. 259.
55. Castel, p. 64.
56. Ibid., pp. 21–22.
57. Ibid., p. 22.
58. Ibid., p. 187.
59. Ibid., p. 190.
60. Castel, p. 64.
61. Phillip S. Foner, *Reconstruction and After*, p. 192.
62. Ibid., p. 193.
63. Ibid., p. 34.
64. Castel, p. 69.
65. Bennett, p. 225.

66. Castel, p. 82–83.
67. Eric Foner, *Reconstruction*, p. 190.
68. Ibid., p. 201.
69. Ibid., p. 206).
70. Ibid., pp. 333–334.
71. Ibid., p. 336.
72. William S. McFeely. *Grant: A Biography* (New York: Norton, 1981), p. 12.
73. Ibid., p. 61.
74. Ibid., p. 62.
75. Ibid., p. 72.
76. DuBois, *Black Reconstruction in America*, p. 683.
77. Kenneth E. Davison. *The Presidency of Rutherford B. Hayes* (Westport, CT: Greenwood Press, 1972), p. 22.
78. Bennett, p. 213.
79. DuBois, *Black Reconstruction in America*, p. 686.
80. Ibid., p. 685.
81. Lawrence Grossman. *The Democratic Party and the Negro: Northern and National Politics, 1868–92* (Urbana: University of Illinois Press, 1976), p. 4.
82. Davison, p. 23.
83. Davison, p. 12.
84. Rayford W. Logan. *The Betrayal of the Negro: From Rutherford B. Hayes to Woodrow Wilson* (New York: Collier, 1955), p. 38.
85. Ibid., p. 42.
86. Allan Peskin. *Garfield: A Biography* (Kent, OH: Kent State University Press), p. 177.
87. Ibid., p. 234.
88. Ibid.
89. Ibid., p. 332.
90. Ibid., p. 333.
91. Justus D. Doenecke. *The Presidencies of James A. Garfield and Chester A. Arthur* (Lawrence: The Regents Press of Kansas, 1981), p. 48; George M. Frederickson. *The Black Image in the White Mind: The Debate on Afro-American Character and Destiny, 1817–1914* (New York: Harper and Row, 1971), p. 185.
92. Doenecke, p. 48.
93. Davison, p. 136.
94. Logan, p. 57.
95. Ibid., p. 55.
96. Ibid., p. 56.
97. Grossman, p. 109.
98. Ibid., p. 144.

99. Harry J. Sievers. *Benjamin Harrison: Hoosier President, the White House and After* (Indianapolis: Bobbs-Merrill, 1968), p. 27.

100. Ibid., p. 150.

101. Frederick Douglass, "The Return of the Democractic Party to Power," in Phillip S. Foner's *Reconstruction and After*, volume IV of *The Life and Writings of Frederick Douglass* (New York: International Publishers, 1955), p. 128.

102. Ibid., p. 129.

103. Phillip S. Foner, *Reconstruction and After*, p. 362.

104. Ibid., p. 128; Logan, p. 63.

105. Logan, pp. 66–70; Homer E. Socolofsky and Allan B. Spetter. *The Presidency of Benjamin Harrison* (Lawrence: University Press of Kansas, 1987), pp. 64–65.

106. Logan, p. 78.

107. Grossman, p. 158.

108. Ibid., p. 160.

109. Logan, pp. 92–93.

110. Ibid., p. 92.

111. Margaret Leech. *The Days of McKinley* (New York: Harper and Brothers, 1959), pp. 1–8.

112. Ibid., p. 34.

113. H. Wayne Morgan. *William McKinley and His America* (Syracuse, NY: Syracuse University Press, 1963), p. 135.

114. Ibid., p. 246.

115. Ida B. Wells-Barnett. *Mob Rule in New Orleans: Robert Charles and His Fight to the Death* (Chicago: Ida B. Wells-Barnett, 1900), pp. 44–45.

116. Logan, p. 97.

117. Ibid., pp. 99–100.

118. Ibid., p. 349.

119. Ibid., pp. 98–99.

120. Ibid., p. 100.

121. Wayne Andrews, editor. *The Autobiography of Theodore Roosevelt* (New York: Scribner's, 1958), p. 15.

CHAPTER FOUR

1. Ann J. Lane. *The Brownsville Affair: National Crisis and Black Reaction* (Port Washington, NY: Kennikat Press, 1971), p. 80.

2. Ibid.

3. Ibid., p. 137.

4. Lewis L. Gould. *The Presidency of Theodore Roosevelt* (Lawrence: University Press of Kansas, 1991), p. 242.

5. Nathan Miller. *Theodore Roosevelt: A Life* (New York: Morrow, 1992), p. 468.

6. Gould, p. 241.
7. Elting E. Morison. *The Letters of Theodore Roosevelt* (Cambridge: Harvard University Press, 1951), p. 1304.
8. Ibid., p. 1305.
9. Andrews, p. 11.
10. Albert Bushnell Hart and Herbert Ronald Ferleger, editors. *Theodore Roosevelt Cyclopedia* (Oyster Bay, NY: Theodore Roosevelt Association, 1989), p. 381.
11. Ibid., p. 379.
12. Henry F. Pringle. *The Life and Times of William Howard Taft*, volume one (Hamden, CT: Archon Books, 1964), p. 390; *The Messenger, Volumes 3–4, 1921–1922* (New York: Negro Universities Press, 1969), p. 236.
13. Paolo E. Coletta. *The Presidency of William Howard Taft* (Lawrence: University Press of Kansas, 1973), p. 30.
14. Logan, p. 360.
15. David J. Hellwig. "The Afro-American Press and Woodrow Wilson's Mexican Policy, 1913–1917," *Phylon*, XLVIII, no. 4 (1987), p. 262.
16. Ronald W. Walters. *Black Presidential Politics in America: A Strategic Approach* (Albany: State University of New York, 1988), p. 11.
17. Kenneth O'Reilly. *'Racial Matters': The FBI's Secret File on Black America, 1960–1972* (New York: The Free Press, 1989), pp. 11–12.
18. Kendrick A. Clements. *Woodrow Wilson: World Statesman* (Boston: Twayne, 1987), pp. 3–7.
19. Henry Wilkinson Bragdon. *Woodrow Wilson: The Academic Years* (Cambridge: The Belknap Press of Harvard University Press, 1967), p. 236.
20. Ibid., p. 237.
21. Kenneth O'Reilly. *Nixon's Piano: Presidents and Racial Politics from Washington to Clinton* (New York: The Free Press, 1995), pp. 85–89.
22. Clements, p. 99.
23. Hellwig, p. 262.
24. Christine Lunardini. "Standing Firm: William Monroe Trotter's Meetings with Woodrow Wilson, 1913–1914," *Journal of Negro History*, 64 (Summer 1979), p. 246.
25. Ibid. p. 248).
26. Ibid., p. 249.
27. Ibid.
28. Ibid., p. 250.
29. Ibid., p.256.
30. Ibid., p. 260.
31. Robert K. Murray. *The Harding Era: Warren G. Harding and His Administration* (Minneapolis: University of Minnesota Press, 1969), p. 397.

32. Reynolds Farley. *Growth of the Black Population: A Study of Democratic Trends* (Chicago: Markham, 1970), p. 23; Eugene P. Trani and David L. Wilson. *The Presidency of Warren G. Harding* (Lawrence: The Regents Press of Kansas, 1977), p. 33.
33. Murray, p. 7.
34. Trani and Wilson, p. 35.
35. Murray, p. 63.
36. Ibid., p. 8.
37. Ibid., p. 64.
38. Ibid.
39. Ibid., pp. 63–64.
40. Ibid., p. 65.
41. Trani and Wilson, p. 58.
42. Ibid., p. 103).
43. *The Messenger*, p. 301.
44. Ibid., p. 302.
45. Ibid., p. 305.
46. Ibid., pp. 275–276.
47. Philip R. Moran, editor. *Calvin Coolidge, 1872–1933, Chronology—Documents—Bibliographical Aid* (Dobbs Ferry, NY: Oceana Publications, 1970), p. 114.
48. C. Bascom Slemp. *The Mind of the President* (Garden City, NY: Doubleday, Page, 1926), p. 246.
49. W. E. B. DuBois. "Is Al Smith Afraid of the South?" *The Nation*, 127 (October 17, 1928), p. 190.
50. Samuel O'Dell. "Blacks, the Democratic Party, and the Presidential Election of 1928: A Mild Rejoinder," *Phylon*, XLVIII, no. 1 (1987), p. 4.
51. Ibid., p. 2.
52. Ibid., p. 4.
53. Ibid.
54. Ibid., p. 7.
55. Ibid., p. 8.
56. Ibid.
57. Ibid., p. 3.
58. Donald J. Lisio. *Hoover, Blacks & Lily-whites: A Study of Southern Strategies* (Chapel Hill: University of North Carolina Press, 1985), p. 87.
59. Allan J. Lichtman. *Prejudice and the Old Politics: The Presidential Elections of 1928* (Chapel Hill: University of North Carolina Press, 1979), p. 150.
60. Lisio, p. 92.
61. David Burner. *Herbert Hoover: A Public Life* (New York: Knopf, 1978), p. 8, 33.

62. Ibid., pp. 197–98.
63. Lisio, pp. 208–209.
64. Ibid., p. 209.
65. Ibid., p. 229.
66. Ibid., pp. 235–236.
67. W. B. Norton, et al. *A People and a Nation* (New York: Houghton Mifflin, 1990), p. 791.
68. Barton J. Bernstein, editor. *Politics and Policies of the Truman Administration* (Chicago: Quadrangle Books, 1970), p. 271; Herbert Garfinkel. *When Negroes March: The March on Washington Movement in the Organizational Politics for FEPC* (New York: Atheneum, 1969), p. 8, 38.
69. Garfinkel, p. 18.
70. Ibid., p. 38.
71. Lisio, p. 268.
72. Raymond Wolters. "The New Deal and the New Negro," in *The New Deal*, edited by Robert Hamlett Bremner and David Brody (Columbus: Ohio State University Press, 1975), p. 170.
73. Matthew Rees. "Father Franklin," *Diversity*, 3 (March/April 1, 1992), pp. 23–28; Wolters, p. 207.
74. Wolters, p. 181.
75. Ralph J. Bunche. *The Political Status of the Negro in the Age of FDR* (Chicago: University of Chicago Press, 1973), p. 608.
76. Wolters, p. 185.
77. John G. Van Deusen. "The Negro in Politics," *Journal of Negro History*, 21 (1936), pp. 273–274.
78. Wolters, p. 172.
79. Bunche, p. 610; Wolters, p. 173.
80. Wolters, p. 174.
81. Ibid., pp. 174–175.
82. Ibid., p. 191.
83. Ibid., p. 192.
84. Garfinkel, pp. 15–16.
85. Walter White. "FDR's Apology," in *The Burden of Race*, edited by Gilbert Osofsky (New York: Harper, 1967), p. 411.
86. O'Reilly, p. 14.
87. Ibid. pp. 18–19.
88. Walter White, p. 409.
89. Frank Freidel. *Franklin D. Roosevelt: A Rendezvous with Destiny* (Boston: Little, Brown, 1990), p. 247; Garfinkel, pp. 15–16.
90. Freidel, p. 605.

CHAPTER FIVE

1. Merle Miller. *Plain Speaking: An Oral Biography of Harry Truman* (New York: Berkley, 1974), p. 155.

2. "Private Letters Reveal Truman Racist Attitudes," *The Washington Times* (October 25, 1991), p. 4.

3. Ibid.

4. Carl T. Rowan. *Breaking Barriers: A Memoir* (New York: Harper-Collins, 1991), p. 164.

5. Joint Committee on Printing. *Memorial Services in the Congress of the United States and Tributes in Eulogy of Harry S Truman, a Late President of the United States* (Washington, DC: U.S. Government Printing Office, 1973).

6. Bernstein, p. 279.

7. Robert Frederick Burk. *The Eisenhower Administration and Black Civil Rights* (Knoxville, TN: University of Tennessee Press, 1984), p. 91; Dorothy K. Newman, et al. *Protest, Politics, and Prosperity: Black Americans and White Institutions, 1940–75* (New York: Pantheon, 1978), p. 12.

8. Newman, et al., p. 12.

9. Bernstein, p. 274.

10. O'Reilly, p. 31.

11. Ibid., p. 40.

12. Martin Bauml Duberman. *Paul Robeson* (New York: Knopf, 1988), p. 363.

13. Burk, p. 14.

14. Bernstein, pp. 287–288.

15. Newman, et al., p. 14; Manning Marable. *Race, Reform, and Rebellion: The Second Reconstruction in Black America, 1945–1982* (Jackson: University Press of Mississippi, 1984), p. 25.

16. Thomas Byrne Edsall. *Chain Reaction: The Impact of Race, Rights, and Taxes on American Politics* (New York: Norton, 1991), p 33; Garfinkel, p. 176.

17. Theodore White. *The Making of the President, 1960* (New York: Atheneum, 1961), p. 233.

18. Newman, et al., p. 3.

19. E. Frederic Morrow. *Black Man in the White House* (New York: Mac-Fadden, 1963), pp. 126–127.

20. Ibid., p. 127.

21. Burk, p. 17.

22. Ibid., p. 18.

23. Ibid., p. 20.

24. Ibid., p. 27.

25. Ibid., p. 28.

26. Ibid., p. 16.

27. Stephen E. Ambrose. *Eisenhower: The President*, volume 2 (New York: Simon and Schuster, 1984), p. 127.

28. Ibid., p. 190.

29. William Manchester. *The Glory and the Dream: A Narrative History of America, 1932–1972* (New York: Bantam, 1974), p. 804.
30. Ambrose, p. 327.
31. Morrow, pp. 47–48.
32. Ibid., pp. 28–30.
33. Ibid., p. 86.
34. Ibid., pp. 176–177.
35. Theodore White. *The Making of the President, 1960*, p. 315.
36. Thomas C. Reeves. *A Question of Character: A Life of John F. Kennedy* (New York: The Free Press, 1991), p. 210; Theodore White. *The Making of the President, 1960*, p. 322.
37. Theodore White. *The Making of the President, 1960*, p. 323.
38. Ibid.
39. Ibid.
40. Walters, *Black Presidential Politics in America*, p. 28.
41. Thomas C. Reeves, p. 119.
42. Carl M. Brauer. *John F. Kennedy and the Second Reconstruction* (New York: Columbia University Press, 1977), p. 16.
43. Theodore C. Sorensen, editor. *"Let the Word Go Forth": The Speeches, Statements, and Writings of John F. Kennedy* (New York: Delacorte, 1988), p. 183.
44. James N. Giglio. *The Presidency of John F. Kennedy* (Lawrence: University Press of Kansas, 1991), p. 177; Sorensen, p. 186.
45. Stephen B. Oates. *Let the Trumpet Sound: The Life of Martin Luther King, Jr.* (New York: Harper and Row, 1982), pp. 158–159.
46. Ibid., pp. 169–170.
47. James Melvin Washington. *A Testament of Hope: The Essential Writings of Martin Luther King, Jr.* (San Francisco: Harper and Row, 1986), pp. 154–155.
48. Oates, *Let the Trumpet Sound*, p. 172.
49. Clayborne Carson. *In Struggle: SNCC and the Black Awakening of the 1960s* (Cambridge: Harvard University Press, 1981), p. 35.
50. Thomas C. Reeves, p. 341.
51. Carson, pp. 34–35.
52. Frances Fox Piven and Richard A. Cloward. *Poor People's Movements* (New York: Vintage, 1979), p. 235; Thomas C. Reeves, p. 338.
53. Oates, *Let the Trumpet Sound*, p. 206–207.
54. Piven and Cloward, p. 231; O'Reilly, p. 50.
55. Piven and Cloward, pp. 232–233.
56. Ibid.; Theodore White. *America in Search of Itself: The Making of the President, 1956–1980* (New York: Harper and Row, 1982), pp. 38–39.
57. Piven and Cloward, p. 235.
58. Carson, p. 85.

59. Thomas C. Reeves, p. 350.
60. Ibid., p. 352.
61. Sorensen, p. 193.
62. Ibid., p. 194.
63. Oates, *Let the Trumpet Sound*, p. 238.
64. Manning Marable. *Black American Politics: From the Washington Marches to Jesse Jackson* (London: Verso, 1985), p. 90.
65. Giglio, p. 187.
66. Malcolm X. *Malcolm X Speaks: Selected Speeches and Statements*, edited by George Breitman (New York: Grove, 1965), p. 14.
67. Ibid., p. 16.
68. Thomas C. Reeves, p. 359.
69. Oates, *Let the Trumpet Sound*, p. 255.
70. Ibid., p. 264.
71. Robert A. Caro. *The Years of Lyndon Johnson: Means of Ascent* (New York: Knopf, 1990), p. 125.
72. Robert Dallek. *Lone Star Rising: Lyndon Johnson and His Times, 1908–1960* (New York: Oxford University Press, 1991), p. 276.
73. Doris Kearns. *Lyndon Johnson and the American Dream* (New York: Harper and Row, 1976), p. 106.
74. Carson, p. 115.
75. Ibid., p. 109.
76. Ibid., p. 123.
77. O'Reilly, p. 186.
78. Carson, p. 125.
79. Malcolm X, p. 110.
80. Joseph A. Califano, Jr. *The Triumph and the Tragedy of Lyndon Johnson* (New York: Simon and Schuster, 1991), p. 55.
81. Theodore White. *The Making of the President, 1964* (New York: Signet, 1965), pp. 174–178.
82. Kearns, p. 192.
83. White, *The Making of the President, 1964*, p. 380.
84. Ibid., p. 362.
85. Califano, pp. 55–57.
86. White. *America in Search of Itself*, p. 109.
87. Califano, pp. 55–57; Edsall, 1991, pp. 83–84.
88. Califano, p. 57.
89. Kearns, p. 305.
90. Ibid., pp. 305–306.
91. Califano, p. 62.
92. Ibid., p. 122.
93. Clarence Lusane. *The Struggle for Equal Education* (New York: Franklin Watts, 1992), p. 84.
94. Ibid., p. 85.

95. Califano, p. 63.
96. *The Kerner Report: The 1968 Report of the National Advisory Committee on Civil Disorders* (New York: Pantheon, 1988), pp. 95–97.
97. O'Reilly, p. 245.
98. Califano, p. 73.

CHAPTER SIX

1. Richard M. Nixon. *The Memoirs of Richard Nixon*, volume 1 (New York: Warner, 1978), p. 304; White, *The Making of the President, 1960*, p. 203.
2. Tom Wicker. *One of Us: Richard Nixon and the American Dream* (New York: Random House, 1991), p. 239.
3. Nixon, p. 24.
4. Wicker, p. 238.
5. Steve Fraser and Gary Gerstile, editors. *The Rise and Fall of the New Deal Order, 1930–1980.* (Princeton, NJ: Princeton University Press, 1989), p. 258.
6. Aaron Singer, editor. *Campaign Speeches of American Presidential Candidates, 1928–1972* (New York: Frederick Ungar, 1976), p. 377.
7. Ibid., pp. 377–379.
8. Ibid., p. 362.
9. Ibid., p. 363.
10. Ibid.
11. Ambrose, p. 332.
12. Theo Lippman, Jr. *Spiro Agnew's America* (New York: Norton, 1972), pp. 141–142; Leon E. Panetta and Peter Gall. *Bring Us Together: The Nixon Team and the Civil Rights Retreat* (New York: Lippincott, 1971), p. 5; Garry Wills. *Nixon Agonistes: The Crisis of the Self-Made Man* (Dunwoody, GA: Norman S. Berg, 1969), p. 261.
13. Lippman, p. 143.
14. Ibid., p. 109.
15. Ibid., p. 112.
16. Panetta and Gall, p. 67.
17. John Osborne. *The Second Year of the Nixon Watch* (New York: Liveright, 1971), p. 22.
18. Ibid., pp. 22–23.
19. Ibid., p. 35.
20. Panetta and Gall, p. 101.
21. Ibid., p. 102.
22. Ambrose, p. 365.
23. Ibid.
24. Ibid.
25. Ibid., p. 523.
26. O'Reilly, p. 261.

27. Ibid., p. 267.
28. Ibid., p. 268.
29. Ibid., pp. 260–268.
30. Ibid., p. 280.
31. Ibid., p. 281.
32. Ibid., p. 302.
33. Ibid., p. 298.
34. Ibid., p. 334.
35. Richard Reeves. *A Ford Not a Lincoln* (New York: Harcourt, Brace and Jovanovich, 1975), pp. 39–40.
36. George J. Lankevich, editor. *Gerald R. Ford, 1913–, Chronology—Documents—Bibliographic Aids* (Dobbs Ferry, NY: Oceana Publications, 1977), p. 18.
37. Ibid., p. 78.
38. Ibid., p. 80.
39. Ibid., p. 82.
40. Thomas Y. Crowell. *Promises to Keep: Carter's First 100 Days* (New York: Crowell, 1977), p. 65.
41. Ibid., p. 70.
42. Ibid., p. 71.
43. Ibid.
44. Ibid., p. 72.
45. James Wooten. *Dasher: The Roots and the Rising of Jimmy Carter* (New York: Summit, 1978), p. 89.
46. Bruce Mazlish and Edwin Diamond. *Jimmy Carter: A Character Portrait* (New York: Simon and Schuster, 1979), p. 30; Wooten, p.91
47. Wooten, p. 97.
48. Ibid., p. 287.
49. Ibid., p. 333.
50. Ibid., p. 351.
51. White, *America in Search of Itself*, p. 206.
52. Mazlish and Diamond, p. 206.
53. Crowell, p.81.
54. Marable, *Race, Reform and Rebellion*, p. 184.
55. Ibid.
56. Chuck Stone. "A Black Scholar Debate: The Jordan-Carter Exchange" and "Carter's Paternalistic Racism and Inept Presidency," *The Black Scholar* (March 1978), p. 40.
57. Ibid., pp. 40–41.
58. Marable, *Race, Reform and Rebellion*, pp. 184–185.
59. White, *America in Search of Itself*, p. 386.
60. Rowan, p. 311.
61. Lee Edwards. *Ronald Reagan: A Political Biography* (Houston: Nordland, 1981), p. 219.

62. Jesse Jackson. "Big Difference between Candidates," *Atlanta Constitution* (November 4, 1980), p. 5-A.

63. White, *America in Search of Itself*, p. 412.

64. Rowan, p. 322.

65. Ronald Reagan. *An American Life* (New York: Simon and Schuster, 1990), p. 30.

66. Edwards, pp. 19–20.

67. Ibid.

68. Ronald Reagan. "The Time for Action Is Now" in *A Time for Choosing: The Speeches of Ronald Reagan, 1961–1982* (New York: Americans for the Reagan Agenda, 1983), p. 277.

69. Dallek, p. 70.

70. Reagan, "The Time for Action Is Now", p. 278.

71. Dallek, p. 79.

72. Rowan, p. 313.

73. "US Sues DC in Hiring Plan," *The Washington Post* (March 12, 1985), p. A4.

74. Lusane, *The Struggle for Equal Education*, p. 98.

75. Laurence I. Barrett. *Gambling with History: Ronald Reagan in the White House* (Garden City, NY: Doubleday, 1983), p. 416.

76. Dallek, p. 82

77. Lusane, *The Struggle for Equal Education*, pp. 97–98.

78. Lorenzo Morris, editor. *The Social and Political Implications of the 1984 Jesse Jackson Presidential Campaign* (New York: Praeger, 1990), pp. 4–5.

79. Frank Watkins and Frank Clemente. *Keep Hope Alive: Jesse Jackson's 1988 Presidential Campaign* (Boston: Keep Hope Alive and South End Press, 1989), p. 6.

80. Walters, p. 26.

81. Elizabeth O. Colton. *The Jackson Phenomenon: The Man, the Power, the Message* (New York: Doubleday, 1989), pp. 83–84.

82. Ibid., p. 86.

83. Watkins and Clemente, p. 10.

84. Ibid., p. 39.

85. Ibid.

86. Ibid.

87. D. H. Swinton. "Economic Status of Black Americans," in *The State of Black America* (New York: Urban League, 1989).

88. Jeffrey M. Elliot. "The 'Willie' Horton Nobody Knows," *The Nation* (August 23/30, 1993), pp. 201–205.

89. Edsall, pp. 223–224.

90. Elliot, p. 207.

91. Clarence Lusane. *Pipe Dream Blues: Racism and the War on Drugs* (Boston: South End Press, 1991), p. 3.

92. "In District's War on Drugs, Bennett Seems to Favor Short-Term Answers, *The Washington Post* (April 16, 1989), p. A25.

93. Lusane, *Pipe Dream Blues*, p. 3.
94. "Despite Achievement, Thomas Felt Isolated," *The Washington Post* (September 9, 1991), A6.
95. Ibid.
96. James Steele. "Beatin' Around the Bush: The Meaning of the Republican Convention for African Americans," *Black Political Agenda '92* (August 1992), p. 1, 4.
97. Marshall Frady. *Jesse: The Life and Pilgrimage of Jesse Jackson* (New York: Random House, 1996), pp. 360–361.
98. Robert C. Smith. *We Have No Leaders: African Americans in the Post–Civil Rights Era* (Albany: State University of New York Press, 1996). p. 221.
99. Pamela Loprest. *Families Who Left Welfare: Who Are They and How Are They Doing?* (Washington, DC: Urban Institute, 1999).
100. William Jefferson Clinton. "One America in the 21st Century," address to the graduating class of the University of California at San Diego, 14 June 1997.

For Further Information

Books

Bassett, J.S. *The Life of Andrew Jackson*, volumes 1 and 2 (New York: Archon Books, 1967; originally published in 1911)

Bell, Malcolm, Jr. *Major Butler's Legacy: Five Generations of a Slaveholding Family* (Athens: The University of Georgia Press, 1987)

Bennett, Lerone. *Before the Mayflower: A History of the Negro in America* (Baltimore: Penguin Books, 1962)

Brodie, Fawn. *Thomas Jefferson: An Intimate History* (New York: Norton, 1974)

Burk, Robert Frederick. *The Eisenhower Administration and Black Civil Rights* (Knoxville: The University of Tennessee Press, 1984)

Caro, Robert A. *The Years of Lyndon Johnson: Means of Ascent* (New York: Knopf, 1990)

Carson, Clayborne. *In Struggle: SNCC and the Black Awakening of the 1960s* (Cambridge, MA: Harvard University Press, 1981)

DuBois, W. E. B. *Black Reconstruction in America* (New York: Atheneum, reprinted 1983)

Edsall, Thomas Byrne. *Chain Reaction: The Impact of Race, Rights, and Taxes on American Politics* (New York: Norton, 1991)

Ferling, John E. *The First of Men: A Life of George Washington* (Knoxville: University of Tennessee Press, 1988)

Foner, Eric. *Reconstruction: America's Unfinished Revolution, 1863–1877* (New York: Harper and Row, 1988)

Foner, Eric, editor. *Nat Turner* (Englewood Cliffs, NJ: Prentice-Hall, 1971)

Freehling, William W. *The Road to Disunion: Volume 1, Secessionists at Bay, 1776–1854* (New York: Oxford University Press, 1990)

Giglio, James N. *The Presidency of John F. Kennedy* (Lawrence: University Press of Kansas, 1991)

Jordan, Winthrop D. *White Over Black: American Attitudes Toward the Negro, 1550–1812* (Baltimore: Penguin Books, 1969)

Katz, William Loren. *Breaking the Chains: African-American Slave Resistance* (New York: Atheneum, 1990)

The Kerner Report: The 1968 Report of the National Advisory Committee on Civil Disorders (New York: Pantheon Books, 1988)

Lane, Ann J. *The Brownsville Affair: National Crisis and Black Reaction* (Port Washington, NY: Kennikat Press, 1971)

Lisio, Donald J. *Hoover, Blacks, & Lily-whites: A Study in Southern Strategies* (Chapel Hill: The University of North Carolina Press, 1985)

Litwack. Leon F. *Been in the Storm So Long: The Aftermath of Slavery* (New York: Vintage Books, 1980)

Logan, Rayford W. *The Betrayal of the Negro: From Rutherford B. Hayes to Woodrow Wilson* (New York: Collier, 1954)

Lusane, Clarence. *Pipe Dream Blues: Racism and the War on Drugs* (Boston: South End Press, 1991)

———. *The Struggle for Equal Education* (New York: Franklin Watts, 1992)

Malone, Dumas. *Jefferson and the Ordeal of Liberty: Volume 3, Jefferson and His Time* (Boston: Little, Brown, 1962)

Marable, Manning. *Black American Politics: From the Washington Marches to Jesse Jackson* (London: Verso, 1985)

Morrow, E. Frederic. *Black Man in the White House* (New York: MacFadden Books, 1963)

Parker, Robert. *Capitol Hill in Black and White* (New York: Jove Books, 1986)

Walters, Ronald W. *Black Presidential Politics in America: A Strategic Approach* (Albany: State University of New York, 1988)

ORGANIZATIONS AND INTERNET SITES

The African-American Journey

http://www.pbs.org/aajourney/

A directory of PBS sites that showcase the unique experiences and accomplishments of African-Americans.

Center for African & African-American Art and Culture

http://www.caaac.org/2.0/

62 Fulton Street

San Francisco, CA 94102

An organization dedicated to the promotion, enhancement, and delivery of African and African-American art and culture.

Gateway to African-American History

http://usinfo.state.gov/usa/blackhis/

Documents, articles, and links honoring and acknowledging the accomplishments of African-Americans. From the U.S. Department of State International Information Program.

Schomburg Center for Research in Black Culture
http://www.nypl.org/research/sc/sc.html
515 Malcolm X Boulevard
New York, NY 10037-1801
A national research library devoted to collecting, preserving, and providing access to resources documenting the experiences of peoples of African descent throughout the world.

INDEX

Numbers in *italics* represent illustrations

Fair Employment Practices Committee, 106, 114
Federal Bureau of Investigation, 128, 130, 131, 135, 134, 141
Federalist Papers, 25
Federalist Party, 17
Fifteenth Amendment, 81, 92
Fillmore, Millard, 53–54
Foraker, Joseph B., 90
Forced emigration idea, 20–21, 26, 30
Ford, Gerald, 143–144
Forten, William D., 67
Fortune, T. Thomas, 82
Franklin, C.A., 118
"Free" blacks, 46
Free Breakfast for Children, 143
Freedmen's Bureau, 75, 78
Freedmen's Monument, 65–66
Freedom of speech, 37–38
Freedom Rides, 124–125
"Free" states, 31–32
Fugitive Slave Act, 53, 54
Fugitive slaves, 44–47
    and Native Americans, 44

Gabriel. *See* Prosser, Gabriel
"Gag rule," 37–38
Garfield, James A., 80–82
Garner, John Nance, 107
Garrison, William Lloyd, 40, *40*, 50
Gell, Monday, 36
"Gentlemen's Agreement" of 1877, 79–80
Ghetto informants, 141, 143
Ghetto riots, 1966, 135
Goodman, Robert, 156
Grant, Ulysses S., 77, 77–79
"Great Exodus," of 1878–1879, 80

Hamer, Fannie Lou, 131
Hampton, Wade, 79
Hanna, Mark, 96
Harding, Warren G., 96–100

Harris, Patricia Roberts, 146
Harrison, Benjamin, 83–85, *84*
Harrison, William Henry, 48–49
Hayes, Rutherford B., 79–80
Hayes-Tilden Compromise, 79–80
Hemings, Sally, 21–22
Henry, Patrick, 11–12
Hermitage Plantation, 41–42
Hill, Anita, 161
Hill, T. Arnold, 108–109
Hooks, Benjamin, 147
Hoover, Herbert, 101–106
Hoover, J. Edgar, 135
Horton, Willie, 158–159
Howard, O.O., 78
Humphrey, Hubert, 138
Humphrey-Hawkins bill, 148
Hunter, David, 59
Hutchinson, Thomas, 11, 17

"I Have a Dream" (speech), 129

Jackson, Andrew, 33, 39–44
Jackson, Jesse, 147, *154*, 154–157
Jackson, Keith, 160
Jefferson, Thomas, 9, 17–25, 32
    and Sally Hemings, 21–22
Jim Crow laws, 24, 85, 116–117
Johnson, Andrew, 68, *70*, 70–76
Johnson, Lyndon B., 130–136, *133*
Johnson, Samuel, 12
Jordan, Vernon, 147
Judge, Oney, 15

Kennedy, John F., 120–129, *126*
Kennedy, Robert F., 124, 125, 127
King, Clennon, 144–145
King, Coretta Scott, 121
King, Martin Luther, Jr., *121*, 121–129, *129*, 135
Ku Klux Klan, 78

Lafayette, Marquis de, 24, *31*
"Lily-white" delegates, 104

ABOUT THE AUTHOR

CHRISTOPHER B. BOOKER has been involved in research on African-American social problems for more than two decades. He received a bachelor of arts in sociology from Wayne State University and a masters of arts in sociology from the University of Michigan. At present, Booker edits *African American Male Research* (*http://www.pressroom.com/~afrimale*) and is researching a book on blacks and the Clinton presidency. His most recent book, '*I Will Wear No Chain': A Social History of African American Males, 1619–1997* (Greenwood Press) is scheduled for publication in the year 2000. In addition, he contributed a chapter in Charles Jones's *The Black Panther Party Reconsidered* (Black Classic Press). Booker has written scores of articles and book reviews for several publications including *Race and Class, The Black World Today, The Guardian, Black Scholar, Black Political Agenda,* and the *Western Journal of Black Studies.*